Foreign Trade and
The World Trade Organization

FOREIGN TRADE AND THE WORLD TRADE ORGANIZATION

By

Dr. M. Lakshmi Narasaiah

M.A., Ph.D.

Professor & Head
Department of Economics
Sri Krishnadevaraya University Post-graduate Centre
Kurnool–518 002
Andhra Pradesh (India)

DISCOVERY PUBLISHING HOUSE
NEW DELHI

First Published–2004
Reprinted - 2014

ISBN 978-81-7141-768-1

Published by:
DISCOVERY PUBLISHING HOUSE
4831/24, Prahlad Street, Ansari Road, Darya Ganj
New Delhi–110 002 (India)
Phone: 23279245 • Fax: 91-11-23253475
e-mail: dphtemp@indiatimes.com

Printed at:
Infinity Imaging Systems
Delhi

PREFACE

The global economy has changed beyond recognition over the last decade. Widespread economic policy reform and in particular trade liberalization have opened up new opportunities for developing countries. In poor countries, however, the consequences of trade liberalization are not always positive. What can the private sector do to respond better and make the most of new trading opportunities? What factors have limited the impact of economic reforms on export performance?

Why have exports from poorer countries failed to increase more rapidly following trade liberalisation? What can be done to improve performance? Research on the response of firms in the private sector to economic reform can underpin new approaches to export promotion for poorer developing countries. For a long time, protective trade policies, poorly performing state-owned industries and state controls over the private sector were blamed for poor export performance in Africa and south Asia. Now that some of these problems have been remedied, other obstacles have come to light.

The effect of economic liberalization and adjustment on the performance of poor countries has been cause for concern. Trade liberalization should increase incentives to export and facilitate business enterprise by encouraging private ownership through privatization and by attracting foreign investment. Macro-economic stability ought to boost business confidence and performance. All these factors should promote exports, offsetting job and income losses caused by the closure or reorganisation of inefficient enterprises and industries yet, although some degree of reform and stability it is without export growth that was expected.

Trade reform and macro-economic stability may be necessary conditions for improved export performance but by them are insufficient. The obstacles to improving export performance are numerous and there is no easy policy answer. The research programme examined export performance at three levels.

- *Regional:* How trade strategies should vary with skills and natural resource endowments
- *National:* Factors influencing the export performance of manufacturing
- *Sectoral:* The performance of particular sectors of the economy.

The East Asian economies have shown that developing countries can complete successfully in global markets. For many, they provide a blueprint for economic growth applicable to many poor countries.

South Asia's comparative advantage lies in its abundant unskilled labour, while Africa's lies in its abundant natural resources. Different export promotion strategies are essential. South Asia's best prospectus are in labour-intensive manufacturing: the region's low level of exports would soar over the next decade if current obstacles to trade were reduced. Africa's exports could also increase but its biggest potential in primary products that need little educated labour and abundant natural resources.

Dr. M. Lakshmi Narasaiah

Contents

1

World Trade Organization

Affirming that "the establishment of the World Trade Organisation (WTO) ushers in a new era of global economic cooperation, reflecting the widespread desire to operate in a fairer and more open multilateral trading system for the benefit and welfare of their people," more than a hundred ministers in the ancient trading crossroads of Marrakesh signed the Final Act of the Uruguay Round and made decisions ensuring a running start for the WTO.

In the ornate Salle Royale of the Palaisdes Congres, the ministers, one by one, signed the Final Act containing 28 agreements and appended to by some 26,000 pages of national tariff and services schedules, which GATT economists estimate will add some US$755 billion to world exports and raise incomes by some $235 billion annually.

Several ministers also signed the new Government Procurement Code that was negotiated in parallel with the Uruguay Round and three other plurilateral agreements: on dairy products, bovine meat and civil aircraft. The ceremony effectively marked the start of the transition from GATT to the WTO.

In the Marrakesh Declaration they had adopted just hours earlier, the Ministers had saluted as "a historic achievement" the conclusion of the round, which strengthen the world economy, lead to more trade, investment, employment and income growth throughout the world". They had also expressed their determination to "resist protectionist pressures of all kinds". In this regard, they pledged, with immediate effect and until the establishment of the WTO, not to "take any trade measures that would undermine or adversely affect the results of the Uruguay Round negotiations or their implementation."

Ministerial Decisions

The establishment of a Preparatory Committee for the WTO was one of the four Decisions taken by ministers. The other three were: the Decision on Acceptance of and Accession to the Agreement Establishing the World Trade Organization; the Decision on Trade and Environment; and the Decision on Organizational and Financial Consequences flowing from Implementation of the Agreement Establishing the WTO.

The Preparatory Committee, to be headed by Mr. Peter Sutherland in his personal capacity, will be in charge of ensuring an orderly transition from the GATT to the WTO. Its remit is to ensure the efficient operation of the WTO immediately as of the date of its establishment. Thus, it will convene and prepare the Implementation Conference, which will decide formally on the date of entry into force of the WTO Agreement.

Opening Ceremonies

"Our meeting here in Marrakesh takes place at the close of the most ambitious trade negotiations in world economic history – we should be proud of this stride towards a more open world which will be, through the dynamism of exchanges between nations and the lifting of barriers and protectionist regulations, a source of prosperity and welfare for the people worldwide," said His Royal Highness the Crown Prince Sidi Mohammed at the opening of the Ministerial Meeting. He stressed that "we all are witnessing here in Marrakesh what will be the legal and institutional pillar of international Trade in the twenty-first century."

The TNC Chairman at Ministerial level, Minister Sergio Abreau Bonilla (Uruguay), opened the Ministerial Meeting by reminding participants that the real effectiveness of the new trade rules depended on the political will of governments. "We must therefore strengthen our determination to honour the commitments which we will assume with the signature of the Final Act," he said. Minister Abreau added: "Behind each signature, there are millions of workers, farmers, industrialists, professionals and businessmen who harbour the hope that the results of the Round will create new horizons for trade, employment and investment and offer better possibilities of tackling poverty and recession, the paving the way for the economic and social development of nations."

Sutherland's Report

"Few trading caravans can have viewed this beautiful city with as much pleasure and as much relief—as ours does. But then very few trading caravans were on the road for more than seven years, and none carried such a priceless cargo. This week you as Ministers will sign the greatest trade agreement in history, one whose benefits span entire continents and a wide range of trade sectors alike," the TNC Chairman at Officials Level, GATT Director-General Peter Sutherland said.

Mr. Sutherland reported that the work of the TNC since the successful conclusion of the Uruguay Round negotiations on 15 December 1993 had been focused on the preparations for the Marrakesh Meeting. First, the Final Act Embodying the Results of the Uruguay Round of Multilateral Trade Negotiations was legally rectified, agreed and circulated to all participants. Secondly, the schedules of market access commitments in goods and services and the MFN exemption lists in services were multilaterally verified for attachment to the Marrakesh Protocol. Thus, the Final Act, rectified and completed by the verified schedules, was now well as trade and investment.

Reflecting on the successful conclusion of the negations, US Trade Representative Michael Kantor said he was "struck by the thin line that separates success and failure .... (but) we succeeded because the ties that bind us together are strong than the forces seeking to pull us apart." He stressed that "our vision of the trading system must be dynamic and able to meet the emerging challenges to our collective global economic growth." Thus, "increasingly, we will address issues related to each other's internal policies, such as competition policy and other domestic regulatory policies, as well as environmental protection and labour standards."

Canada's Trade Minister, Mr. Roy MacLaren, emphasized that when WTO is asked to tackle new trade policy issues, it should proceed in a manner consistent with its competence and mandate. He warned that "when examining new issues, we must, for example be wary of being seduced by the argument that differing approaches to issues such as environmental protection constitute an unfair trade practice justifying some form of action-new issues can become a vehicle for new protectionism." Minister MacLaren stressed that "to fall victim in the World Trade Organisation to the narrow interest groups who favour trade sanctions as the instrument of choice to force nations to comply with the policies of other would be to abandon some of the most fundamental gains we have made."

Development Goals

India's Minister of Commerce, Mr. Pranab Mukherjee, warned that the acute differences between levels of development and incomes among nations have "enough latent heat to melt down the most elaborately engineered structures." Thus, "the long-term survival of the multilateral trading system will depend upon reducing the present inequities." Regarding new issues, Minister Mukherjee said while India was strongly committed to internationally-recognized labour standards, it could not see any merit in linking this subject to international trade. On the other hand, he attached importance to an examination in the Preparatory Committee of the relationship between immigration policies and international trade.

Bangladesh Minister for Commerce, Mr. M. Shamsul Islam, speaking on behalf of the least-developed countries, hoped that "in the implementation of the Uruguay Round Agreements, the international community will be more responsive to the needs of the most disadvantaged group of nations." He urged a comprehensive assessment of the

Uruguay Round results with "any imbalances...to be redressed through appropriate action including additional trade preferences, development assistance and debt relief." Minister Islam pointed to the "need by LLDCS for substantial technical assistance in the implementation of the results of the Round. On new issues, he supported the consideration of the relationship between movements of natural persons and international trade in the Preparatory Committee.

Zimbabwe's Minister of Industry and Commerce, Dr. H. Murerwa, said that his country's preliminary evaluation of the Uruguay Round results suggested gains for certain products, stand-still position for others and potential losses for some products as a result of erosion of EC trade preferences. However, he believed that "the process of liberalization will in the long-run strengthen the global trading system and benefit the peoples of both the developed and developing countries." Minister Murerwa said the challenge facing the developing countries is "to expand and diversify our export capabilities as well as strengthening the international competitiveness of our products." Re-ready for signature by Ministers. Simultaneously, the TNC at official level had approved for adoption by Ministers four Decisions and the Marrakesh Declaration.

The GATT Director-General said that "the signature ceremony will be a just cause for celebration not only because its represents signing-off on the Uruguay Round, but because it will be signing-on to the work of putting the results into effect and ensuring that their potential is used to the fullest."

Early Ratification Urged

Many Ministers underlined the urgency of ratifying the Uruguay Round agreements to enable the World Trade Organization to be fully operational.

EC Commissioner Sir Leon Brittan emphasized that: "each of us, by our signature at Marrakesh, pledges himself or herself to submit the results of the Uruguay Round for formal approval in accordance with our domestic laws and, equally important, to proceed without delay to implement in our domestic laws, the commitments we made during the negotiations" He said one proof of the quality of those commitments was "the ever-lengthening queue of candidates for accession to the GATT and to the WTO." The EC Commissioner suggested that the WTO tackle the following issues: ensuring intensive cooperation between the WTO and the IMF and the World Bank; addressing urgently the interface between trade and the environment; working with the International Labour Office and other organizations, the WTO must address problems such as child exploitation, forced labour or the denial to workers of free speech or free association; and distortion of trade which can be caused by different standards of competition law and practice in different countries.

Japan's Deputy Prime Minister for Foreign Affairs Mr. Tsutomu Hata, underlined the importance of the Round's conclusion "in securing confidence in the world economic order." He recalled that his country had made significant contributions to the Round, including acceptance of the Agreement on Agriculture and cutting average tariffs on industrial and mining products by 61 per cent to rate as low as 1.5 per cent. "As a result of the Uruguay Round, the Japanese market offers greater opportunities for success by foreign exporters depending upon their efforts," he added. Minister Hata expressed strong support for the early entry into force of the WTO consider additional issues closely related to trade, including regionalism as grading the WTO, he viewed "Marrakesh as the stating platform which will put in place a strong rule-based multilateral trading system that should safeguard the interest of all nations, weak and strong."

The Swiss Minister of Public Economy, Mr. J.P. Delamuraz, pointed out that "by concluding the Uruguay Round, we have taken a decisive step towards the adaptation of the multilateral trading system to contemporary economic realities." This had meant for many participant "substantial adjustments" in domestic economic policy, and for Switzerland reforms in its agricultural policy. "We have added a number of stones to the foundations of a system of multilateral management of the world economy," said Mr. Delamuraz, "we have also recognize the interdependence that is binding us ever more closely together." He noted with special satisfaction the confirmation in the Marrakesh Declaration of the "need for positive measures on behalf of the developing countries, and especially of the least developed among them, as well as the desirability of possible additional measures for their benefit." Mexico's Secretary for Trade and Industrial Development, Mr. Jaime Serra Puche, lauded the result of the Round as signifying "recognition" of the adjustment measures that have been taken up by many developing countries to open their economies. He believed that the results "will further the creation of new jobs and growth in the wage levels of our workers." Secretary Puche stressed that "protection of the environment and workers' rights must go hand in hand with efforts to liberalize world trade, for progress in liberalization to improve the environment and the well-being of workers," but warned against these subject being used as pretexts for "desguised trade protectionism."

Brazil's Minister of External Relations, Mr. Celso Amorium, said that the Uruguay Round "will be remembered as the first one in which developing countries had an active participation in the course of the whole negotiating process." He underlined that "We, the developing countries, have bet on trade liberalization and on the multilateral trading system ... Even though our organization does not bear the word development in its name, it will lose much of its purpose if its rules and disciplines do not contribute to freeing hundreds of millions of human beings from poverty and misery."

The Czech Republic's Minister of Industry and Trade, Mr. Vladimir Dlouhy, highlighted the importance his country attached to "the full integration of the economies in transition into the multilateral trading system." Pointing to these countries' need for better access to markets and fair application of trade and competition rules, he urged that the "the role of the multilateral trading system in this process should be made more effective and more visible.

Singapore's Minister for Trade and Industry, Mr. Yeo Cheow Tong, said " the signing of the Final Act does not mean the end... the challenge now is to see through the successful establishment of the WTO and the implementation of the agreement." Minister Yeo said that Singapore fully supported the WTO because it "has long recognized that the free market system is the way to economic growth and prosperity for our people." In line with this, he extended his country's invitation to host the first Ministerial Meeting of the WTO. "This will be the first time a major global trade meting will be held in Asia, and will complete the circle of Uruguay Round meetings that began in South America in uruguay, then moved on to North America, to Europe and today in Marrakesh, Africa," he added.

Conclusion

At the conclusion of the Ministerial Meeting Minister Abreau noted that many of the one hundred ministers who have spoken had stressed that "notwithstanding the tumultuous economic and political events of the past seven-and-a-half years, all participants have undertaken considerable efforts to improve conditions of market access." Noteworthy too had been "the engagement of the developing and least-developed countries in the process of contributing their share to the global effort to reduce trade barriers."

Another major theme was "the role that multilateral cooperation must play as the foundation for trade relations amongst nations." Min. Abreau said that to implement this principle on a permanent basis, "all had agreed that the results of the negotiations constituted a single undertaking, based on the WTO as a new international institution." He added that one Decision taken at the meeting was the convening of an Implementation Conference later in the year.

In the course of the meeting, the TNC Chairman said ministries had stressed the importance they attached to the examination in the Preparatory Committee of the following subjects for inclusion in the WTO agenda: the relationship between the trading system and internationally recognized labour standards; the relationship between immigration policies and international trade; trade and competition policy, including rules on export financing and restrictive business practices; trade and investment; regionalism; the interaction between trade policies and policies relating to financial and monetary matters, including debt and commodity markets; international trade and company law; the establishment of a mechanism for compensation for the erosion of preference; the link between trade, development, political stability and the alleviation of poverty; and unilateral or extra territorial trade measures.

2

Give Developing Countries a More Favourable Deal

An Assessment of the World Trade Conference in Doha

At the end of the 4th WTO Ministerial Conference in Doha, Qatar, the representatives of all WTO member states vigorously applauded Director-General Mike Moore when he dubbed the adopted work programme for the new round of trade negotiations the "Doha development agenda."

The launching of a new round of trade negotiations with a broad agenda was the objective persistently pursued by the industrial countries, in particular the European Union, the United States, Canada and Japan. This objective has been achieved. Besides the continuation of the negotiations in the fields of agriculture and services, the Ministerial Declaration adopted by the Conference provides for the opening of negotiations in eleven additional fields. Undoubtedly a success for the industrial countries.

CLEAR MANDATE FOR A NEW DEVELOPMENT ROUND

The negotiating mandate, though, clearly reflects the political will to make the new round a "development round" with the aim of significantly improving the integration of the developing countries into the world trading system. To a large extent it takes into account the specific interests of the developing countries. Certainly a success with which the developing countries can credit themselves. A crucial factor for the course and the successful outcome of the Ministerial

Conference was, without doubt, the active involvement of the developing countries in the preparatory and negotiating process.

DOHA DETERMINES MERELY THE WORK PROGRAMME FOR NEGOTIATIONS

The Ministerial Declaration adopted at the conference merely determines the work programme for the new round of trade negotiations. Three factors contributed decisively to the positive outcome of the Ministerial Conference. There was a broad consensus among the WTO member states that *(i)* a second Seattle-like failure would put the WTO's workability at risk and was to be avoided at all costs (the 3rd WTO Ministerial Conference I Seattle in December 1999 ended in chaos without the adoption of a Ministerial Declaration); (*ii*) the recessionary trends in the world economy were to be countered with the successful conclusion of the Ministerial Conference in Doha to improve the prospects for short-term recovery and, thereafter, sustained economic growth; (*iii*) in response to the terrorist attacks of September 11, 2001, there should be a clear commitment to strengthen the rules-based multilateral trading system. Failure was, therefore, not an option. The strategic conclusion drawn from the Seattle failure was to limit the Doha Ministerial Declaration to establishing a broad, generally-worded negotiating mandate for a new round of trade talks that does not anticipate the outcome of the negotiations on controversial issues. The strategy worked. The deliberations at the Ministerial Conference focused on the scope of the negotiating mandate. The task of reconciling the conflicting interests between industrial and developing countries and working out a fair compromise has been left to the forthcoming negotiations.

RECOGNITION OF THE INTERESTS OF THE DEVELOPING COUNTRIES

In view of the objective of creating a basis for sustained economic growth in the developing countries by better integrating them into the world economy and increasing their share in world trade, important preliminary decisions with regard to the forthcoming negotiations were taken by the Ministerial Conference:

- the Ministerial Declaration stresses the importance of implementing and interpreting the Agreement on Trade-Related Aspects of Intellectual Property Rights (TRIPS Agreement) in a manner supportive of public health and access to medicines; in recognition of the seriousness of the problem, a separate 'Declaration on the TRIPS Agreement and Public Health' was adopted; a number of public-health-related issues have been referred to the Council for TRIPS for further deliberation;
- the Council for TRIPS has been tasked to examine the relationship between (*i.*) the TRIPS Agreement and the Convention on Biological Diversity and (*ii.*) the protection of traditional knowledge, taking full account of the development dimension;
- numerous problems regarding the implementation of WTO agreements are dealt with in separate 'Decision on Implementation-Related Issues and Concerns' adopted by the Ministerial Conference; outstanding implementation issues are to be addressed as a matter of priority by the relevant WTO bodies;
- the Council for Trade in Goods will examine the proposal to bring forward the liberalization of the textile sector under the Agreement on Textiles and Clothing;
- as regards agriculture, comprehensive negotiations were agreed on, aiming at: substantial improvements in market access; reductions of, with a view to phasing out, all forms of export subsidies; and substantial reductions in trade-distorting domestic support;
- as regards market access for non-agricultural goods, negotiations were agreed on, with the aim of reducing or, as appropriate, eliminating tariffs and non-tariff trade barriers, in particular on products of export interest to developing countries;

- recognition of the principle of special and differential treatment of the developing countries as an integral part of all WETO agreements;
- technical cooperation and capacity building have been recognized in the Ministerial Declaration as ' core elements of the development dimension of the multilateral trading system' and firm commitments have been established in various paragraphs.

TURNING THE MINISTERIAL DECLARATION'S SPIRIT INTO PRACTICAL POLICY

With these preliminary decisions regarding the agenda of the forthcoming negotiations, the course is set for the better integration of the developing countries into the world economy. To stay the course, there must be clear commitment and political will on the part of the industrial countries to make the new round a 'development round' by taking the developing countries' interests fully into account, being prepared to make meaningful concessions, and making good on the promise of significantly increased trade and investment-related technical assistance.

In the course of the negotiations it might prove a problem that many of the obligations in favour of the developing countries are formulated rather vaguely. The Ministerial Declaration is confined to declarations of intent even where – with a certain degree of goodwill – binding commitments would have been politically feasible. The bringing forward of the liberalization of the textile sector, a key demand of the developing countries, has been referred to the Council for Trade in Goods for examination; this is certainly an expression of the industrial countries' willingness to compromise, but it in no way anticipates the final decision. As regards the objective of duty-free and quota-free access for all products of the least developed countries to the markets of the industrial countries the Ministerial Declaration simply repeats the commitment which was already expressed in the United Nations Millennium Declaration of September 2000, at the 3rd United Nations Conference on Least Developed Countries in Brussels in May 2001, and at the G7/8 Summit in Genoa in July 2001. Except for the European Union, no party has put this commitment into practice so far; the United States and Japan in particular have shown little enthusiasm for introducing duty-free and quota-free access for all LDC products.

What makes us believe that the Doha Ministerial Declaration will make a difference? The chapter on agriculture is more specific in that it provides for negotiations aimed at significantly improved market access, reductions/phasing out of all forms of export subsidies, and substantial reductions in trade-distorting domestic support. However, a clear road map including a timetable for the negotiations and specific benchmarks for the reduction targets were beyond Doha's reach; in addition, the qualifier that the commitment to comprehensive negotiations does not prejudge the outcome of these negotiations leaves a back door open. In conclusion: If you remove the merely rhetorical phrases – such as "we place the developing countries' needs and interests at the heart of the World Programme adopted in this Declaration", "to take fully into account the development dimension ....", - from the Ministerial Declaration, it becomes quite clear that the text contains relatively few 'programming elements' with a view to the development agenda of the forthcoming negotiations.

Fears that the vested interests of the industrial countries will re-gain precedence over development aspects in the course of the negotiating process are certainly not entirely baseless. The 'steel war' the United States is about to declare on the rest of the world clearly indicates that the Doha fair weather period is over. Business as usual has returned. The American steel tariff threats prompted EU Trade Commissioner Pascal Lamy to speak of a "perverse signal at a time when the ink is barely dry on the Doha Agreement."

The non-governmental organizations have a decisive role to play. It is their role to monitor the new round of trade negotiations, to make the negotiating process more transparent, to create public awareness with regard to the issues at stake, and to build up political pressure with the objective of making sure that development aspects are not pushed to one side and that the interests of the developing countries will make their way into the agreements to be concluded.

COHERENCE OF TRADE POLICY AND DEVELOPMENT POLICY

The negotiating mandate for the new round of trade talks adopted in Doha has brought development politics onto the agenda of the WTO. The mention of development aspects in the WTO set of rules and regulations is not, in essence, new. In fact, the development dimension is recognized as an integral part of the general WTO mandate to foster economic growth. However, the particular importance the Doha Ministerial Declaration attaches to the consideration of development aspects in the negotiation process (it seeks, as it is put there, "to place the developing countries' needs and interests at the heart of the work programme") offers the opportunity to achieve greater coherence of trade policy and development policy. In this respect, the Doha Ministerial Declaration reflects the same trend as the "Everything-but-Arms-Initiative"(EBA) of the European Union. Subsequent to its adoption by the EU member states, Pascal Lamy emphasized the coherence aspect as the characteristic feature of the EBA Initiative (outweighing the shortcomings relating to bananas, rice and sugar) by saying, "It is the first time that the European Union's trade policy has been substantially modified by the necessity of contributing to development policy." This perspective also characterized the 3rd United Nations Conference on Least Developed Countries in Brussels in May 2001.

To sum up, it can be said that the Doha conference has sent out an important signal for the process of coordinating trade and development policy with the long-term objective of achieving a coherent policy framework. The next step towards greater coherency can be taken at the International Conference on Financing for Development in Monterrey/ Mexico in March 2002.

SUSTAINABLE DEVELOPMENT AS THE GUIDELINE FOR FURTHER DEVELOPING THE MULTILATERAL TRADING SYSTEM

The Ministerial Declaration reaffirms the commitment to the objective of sustainable development, as stated in the preamble to the Marrakesh Agreement of April 1994 (i.e. the Agreement establishing the WTO). However, theory and practice are far apart. The negotiating mandate for the new round is too cautious a step towards integrating environmental and social aspects into the WTO set of rules and regulations to be able to bridge that gap. Looking at the three pillars of the sustainable development concept – economic development, environmental protection, and social protection – in a nutshell the following can be said:

The negotiating mandate for the new round deserves good grades as far as the first pillar, economic development, is concerned. The course is set for better integration of the developing countries into the multilateral trading system, thus giving them the chance of actually benefiting from further trade liberalization in the form of trade-induced economic growth. The inclusion of the so-called 'Singapore issues', investment and competition, offers the prospect of a medium to long-term improvement of the business and investment climate in the developing countries. As for environmental protection, negotiations on a (very) limited scale have been agreed on, the desirability of further negotiations will be examined. This is certainly not a big breakthrough, but a first step towards integrating ecological aspects into the trade rules. Disappointingly (but not surprisingly), social issues were not dealt with at the Doha Ministerial Conference. The developing countries' resistance to even discussing social issues, such as core labour standards, in the frame-work of the WTO could not be overcome; the issue was considered an absolute 'deal-breaker'.

OUTLOOK

The developing countries' consent to the launching of a new round of trade talks cannot disguise the fact that there are still significant differences of opinion over a number of issues, including such key issues as agriculture, environment, investment and competition, and that there is a great deal of mistrust on the part of the developing countries. The one-day extension of the Ministerial Conference alone is proof of how difficult the process of reaching consensus on the launching of a new round of trade talks and its agenda had been. In order to successfully conclude the new round the of trade talks and its agenda had been. In order to successfully conclude the new round, the industrial countries have to deliver on their commitments, such as improving market access for goods of export interest to the developing countries and increasing their trade-related technical assistance.

The assurance of increased technical assistance was a major bargaining chip in getting the development countries' OK for the new round. If insufficient funds for technical assistance and capacity building measures are provided, it will most certainly diminish the chances of getting quick results. In a comment on the forthcoming negotiations, the British Economist also highlighted the credibility aspect and the need for significant concessions, "Poor countries remain deeply suspicious of the rich world's commitment to truly freer trade. They bitterly remember the Uruguay round, whose benefits went most to the rich. For the new talks to succeed, those suspicions must be proven wrong. Europe and America must quickly open up their markets for farm products and textiles. They must show that environmental concerns are not going to become a backdoor excuse for renewed protectionism. They must reform their oft-abused system of anti-dumping rules. And they must deliver on promises to beef up poorer countries' capacity to deal with the intricate procedures in the world trading system."

The Doha Ministerial Declaration offers the prospect of long-term gains for the developing countries. However, turning potential into actual gains requires tenacity in pursuing policies aimed at improving the business climate and, in general, the framework conditions for economic growth. Increased trade-related technical assistance and improved market access will not automatically result in growing export volumes for the developing countries. In addition, the strengthening and diversification of productive capacity is required. Successful integration into the global economy depends on tackling the supply-side constraints and other 'behind-the-border impediments to trade' (ranging from weak infrastructure, insufficient ancillary services and poor governance to macro-economic instability). The Tanzanian Trade Minister, Iddi Simba, emphasized the complexity of the problems the developing countries are facing in his statement at the Ministerial Conference: "To operationalise the development agenda we need to have adequate capacity building which will go beyond addressing the normal WTO obligations. Adequate resources in the form of financial and technology transfer need to be in place to address the supply-side constraints. Along the same lines, WTO Director-General Mike Moore stated, "Capacity problems [in producing goods and services competitively], not trade barriers, are the major obstacles to growth in developing countries."

CONCLUDING REMARK

By creating a rules-based multilateral trading system, the WTO set of rules and regulations contributes to the shaping of the process of globalization and to the emerging system of global governance. However, it can hardly be disputed that so far the industrial countries have been the main beneficiaries of the WTO-driven economic globalization. We are still miles away from a true win-win situation. In a recent interview with the German weekly *Die Zeit,* the Nigerian President, Olusegun Obasanjo, criticized the industrial countries' hypocrisy, saying "Globalization is a good thing. But only if there is a level playing field, from which all countries are able to benefit. You tell us that we have to open up our markets for your goods, whereas you keep your markets closed for our goods. Europe protects itself with innumerable trade barriers, everybody knows that. What kind of rules are those?"

That is exactly what matters. The new round of trade negotiations launched in Doha must result in modified trade rules. Trade rules which take account of the specific economic constraints of the developing countries and are more favourable to them. The developing countries must be given the chance to 'cash in' on trade liberalization and strengthened by trade-induced economic growth, to pursue national pro-poor policies aimed at eradicating poverty.

3

WTO and India

In order to boost the World trade and help the developing countries to improve their economy, a number of global economic Institutions have been formed to carry out multilateral free trade in a world of multi-lingual and multi-religious community. The main Institutions that form part of global economic Institutions are General Agreement on Tariff and Trade (GATT) or, World Trade Organisation (WTO), United Nations Conference on Trade and Development (UNCTAD), International Monetary Fund (IMF) and the International Bank for Re-construction and Development (IBRD)—World Bank. Hence, WTO provides a forum to the member countries where international trade problems can be discussed and trading opportunities are enlarged.

So far, enough research work has not been carried out on WTO and its implications on selected sectors of Indian economy; hence a need has been felt to carry out a detailed research on *World Trade Organisation : its implications on selected sectors of economy: Agriculture, Textiles and Clothing.*

GATT

GATT is a multi-lateral treaty among the member countries that lays down a certain agreed rules for conducting international trade. The member countries contribute together to four fifth of the total world trade. It is interesting to note that underdeveloped countries form a sizable majority in GATT.

The basic aim of GATT is to liberalize world trade negotiations among member countries, and for the last forty seven years it has been concerned with negotiations on the reduction, even the elimination of trade barriers, tariffs and non-tariffs between countries and improving trade relations so that the international trade flows freely and swiftly. It also provides a forum to member countries to discuss their trade, problems and negotiate to enlarge their trading opportunities.

GATT was formed in the year 1948 and India is its founder member. There were 122 member countries, the majority of which were under developed or developing countries, which were parties to GATT. It is in the interest of the developing countries like India to have more trade with other countries.

There had been seven rounds of negotiations of GATT countries including the general negotiations that were aimed at reducing tariff and non-tariff barriers to the exchange of goods in the course of international trade. The sixth round (1964-67) is known as the Kennedy Round who concentrated on four problems:

- Progressive reduction up to 50% in place of all items except a few products.
- Inclusion of agricultural as well as Industrial Products;
- Discussion on non-tariff obstacles as well as customs duty;
- Non-reciprocity for economically less developed countries.

The seventh round (1973-79) is also known as the Tokyo Round. The highlight of the negotiations was a code on subsidies and countervailing duties. The code was not signed by all the nations but it was a signal to others for its departure from the Most Favoured Nations (MFN) principle.

FINAL ACT

The Uruguay Round of multilateral trade negotiations was concluded on 15 December 1993 after seven years of protracted negotiations. This has been the most complex and controversial of the eight rounds of negotiations by GATT since its inception in 1947. 'The Final Act' was signed on April 15, 1994 at Marrakesh in Morocco. The agreement has come into force on January 1, 1995. The Uruguay Round marks a watershed, and for the first time, multilateral trade negotiations under GATT encompass not only the traditional goods sector but also extend to four new areas, i.e.:

- Agriculture
- Intellectual property rights (IPR) (Particularly product patents and in plants and medicines)
- Textiles and clothing
- Trade in services

The Final Act strings together 25 agreements, declarations and decisions in the goods sector alone, including agreements on Trade Related Aspects of Investment Measures (TRIMS), Trade Related Aspects of Intellectual Property Rights (TRIPS), General Agreement on Trade in Services (GATS) and the agreement on establishing the World Trade Organisation (WTO). With the formal establishment of WTO the wheel will come a full circle in the sense that the troika of international economic institutions envisaged of the Second World War, namely the IMF, IBRD and the International Trade Organization (ITO) will be complete.

The major areas of interest and concern to us in the Uruguay Round are Agriculture, TRIPS, TRIMS, textiles, and tariffs, trade rules and services.

RESULTS OF THE FINAL ACT

As multilateral negotiations generally involve compromises, the results do not always meet the expectations of individual countries. It is often said that no country leaves the negotiating table as a winner or a loser. On the whole, however, the negotiations have brought about positive outcomes. In particular, they have results in:

- An improved framework of multilateral rules governing international trade;

- Further improvements in access to foreign markets for both goods and services.

One of the other achievements of the Round is the establishment of the WTO. The GATT has ceased to be a separate institution and has become part of WTO. The organization is responsible for overseeing the implementation of the multilateral trade rules. The improved mechanism that has been adopted for consultations among member countries on further trade liberalization and for the elaboration of rules in other areas with an international trade.

AGREEMENT ON AGRICULTRE

In the past the Rules of GATT were not always applied fully in the agricultural sectors. Some developed countries in particular protected their costly and inefficient production of temperate zone agricultural products (wheat and other grains, meat and dairy products) by imposing in addition to high tariffs, quantitative restrictions and/or variable levels on imports. This level of protection often resulted in increased domestic production which, because of high prices, could be disposed of in international market only under subsidy. Such subsided sales depressed international prices. They also too away from competitive producers their legitimate market shares.

The Agreement on Agriculture, negotiated in the Uruguay Round, aims at ensuring that basic GATT rules are applied by all countries to trade in agriculture products. The negotiations undertaken in pursuance of these rules have resulted in some progress in the liberation of trade in these products. The agreement has also established a mechanism for future negotiations on the further liberalization of this trade.

Thus the developed countries have agreed to replace quantitative restrictions and other non-tariff measures on agricultural products with tariffs. The new terrified rates as well as other tariffs are to be reduced by 30%. For their part, developing countries and economies in transition have agreed to cut their tariffs by nearly two-thirds of this average. In addition, all countries have bound all tariffs applicable to agricultural products. In most cases, however, developing countries have given bindings at rates that are higher than their current applied or reduced rates. The countries using subsidies, mostly the developed ones have agreed to reduce both production and export subsidies.

AGREEMENT ON TEXTILES AND CLOTHING

Another important agreement of the Uruguay Round is the decision to phase out restrictions on imports of textiles and clothing. These restrictions were imposed by developed countries mainly on imports from developing countries. Under bilateral agreements negotiated under Multi-Fibre Arrangements (MFA), which provided an exception to the GATT Rules prohibiting the use of discriminatory quantitative restrictions. The Agreement on Textiles and Clothing (ATC) which now replaces MFA provides for the removal of restrictions on Textiles in four phases over a period of 10 years. This phasing out will end on 1st January, 2005. From then on, the trade in textiles will be completely integrated into GATT 1994 and will be governed by its rules.

The textiles and clothing sector has remained beyond the pale of GATT disciplines for over two decades now. Its integration into GATT has been a major objective for us in the Uruguay Round, since this sector accounts for nearly 30 per cent of our exports. In 1993-94 our exports in this sector has been of the order of US $ 7.4 billion. Our quota problems under the Multi-Fibre Arrangement (MFA) exist with six countries now, namely, USA, EEC, Canada, Finland, Norway and Austria. They (especially USA and EU) account for nearly two-thirds of the world trade in textiles and clothing.

WTO ON AGRICULTURE

The WTO, which emerged after several rounds of Uruguay Round of negotiations under GATT, has important implications for the agriculture sector in India. Agriculture sector carries the burden of supporting 2/3rd of its population and contributes about 30 per cent of the GDP. The primary objective of this essay is to provide an overall framework for understanding how India must fashion its strategies to achieve international competitiveness in Agriculture sector based on the implications of WTO.

AGRICULTURAL PRODUCTION

Before finding out the competitive advantage of Agricultural Sector we examine country's agricultural production of various products. Given the size of the land area and population, Indian agriculture is one of the largest in the world. It is among the top three producers of rice, cotton, groundnut, tobacco, tea, sugar and milk. But its productivity in terms of output per land area is one of the lowest in the world. The details of the agricultural production in the world and yield per hectare/k.g. are given in the Table 1 and 2. Production of foodgrains and commercial crops in India are given in Table 3.

Table—1 Agricultural Production

(Million tonnes)

	1995		*1992*		*Remarks*
	India	*World*	*India*	*World*	
Wheat	8.0	256.0	55.1	565.1	
Rice	46.3	226.0	109.5	527.7	
Cotton (Lint)	0.8	10.0	2.2	17.7	
Sugarcane	71.6	536.7	249.0	1103.0	
Groundnut	4.9	14.1	8.2	24.3	
Tea	235.0	910.0	703.0	2479.0	Thousand tonnes

Source: CMIE, World Economy and India's Place in it–1994.

Table—2 Agricultural Yield per hectare

(In k.g)

	1980		*1992*		*Remarks*
	India	*World*	*India*	*World*	
Rice	1858	2607	2752	3571	
Wheat	1545	2397	1863	2562	
Cereals	1324	1940	2196	2706	
Pulses	461	579	669	804	

Source: CMIE, World Economy and India's Place in it–1994.

Table—3 Production of Foodgrains and Commercial Crops

(Million Tonnes)

Crop	*1991-92*	*1992-93*	*1993-94*	*1994-95*	*1995-96*		*1996-97*	
					Target	*Final*	*Target*	*Likely*
1	**2**	**3**	**4**	**5**	**6**	**7**	**8**	**9**
Rice	74.7	72.9	80.3	81.8	80.0	79.6	81.0	79.6
Wheat	55.7	57.2	59.8	65.8	60.0	62.6	65.0	64.5
Coarse Cereals	26.0	36.6	30.8	293.9	36.5	29.6	32.5	33.1
Pulses	12.0	12.8	13.3	14.0	15.5	13.2	15.0	14.0
Foodgrains	168.4	179.5	184.3	191.5	192.0	185.0	193.5	191.2
Kharif	91.6	101.5	100.4	101.0	107.5	98.2	104.0	103.2
Rabi	76.8	78.0	83.9	90.4	84.5	86.8	89.5	88.8
Oil Seeds	18.6	20.1	21.5	21.3	22.5	22.4	23.0	24.1
Sugarcane	254.0	228.0	229.7	275.5	255.0	283.0	270.0	273.6
Cotton @	9.7	11.4	10.7	11.9	13.0	13.1	13.0	14.3
Jute & Mesta $	10.3	8.6	8.4	9.1	9.3	8.9	9.0	9.2

(Contd...)

Table—3 (Contd...)

1	2	3	4	5	6	7	8	9
Percentage variation in production over the previous year								
Rice	0.5	–2.4	10.2	1.9		–2.7		0.0
Wheat	1.1	2.7	4.5	10.0		–4.9		3.0
Coarse Cereals	–20.5	40.8	–15.8	–2.9		–1.0		11.8
Pulses	–16.1	6.7	3.9	5.3		–5.7		6.1
Foodgrains	–4.5	6.6	2.7	3.9		–3.4		3.3
Kharif	–7.8	10.8	–1.1	0.6		–2.8		5.1
Rabi	–0.3	1.6	7.6	7.7		–3.9		1.3
Oil Seeds	0.0	8.1	7.0	–0.9		5.2		7.6
Sugarcane	5.4	–10.2	0.7	19.9		2.7		–3.3
Cotton @	–1.0	17.5	–6.1	11.2		10.1		9.2
Jute & Mesta $	12.0	–16.5	–2.3	8.3		-2.2		3.4

@ Million Bales of 170 kg each $ Million Bales of 180 kg each

Source: Economic Survey of India 1996-97.

WTO on Textiles and Clothing

Textile and clothing sector remained the scope of the GATT for the last two decades. It has not been discussed in the first seven rounds of GATT talks. Even in the eighth round, separate treatment has been given to textile and clothing sector, since it was expected that eventual integration of this sector in GATT would require longer period because autonomous adjustments in the industry cannot be made in short run. Presently the textile and clothing trade is governed by the Multi Fibre Agreement (MFA)known as the International Arrangement on Trade and Textiles (IATT). This essay provides an overall framework to find the implications of WTO on Textiles and Clothing Sector in India.

NATIONAL PERSPECTIVE

India's economy depends upon 30% of Textiles and Clothing Industry. This industry employs more than 1/3rd of country's population both skilled and unskilled. The details of textiles and clothing sectors are given in the succeeding paragraphs.

TEXTILES

Cotton Textile industry is the oldest industry in India having made its impact some 150 years back when cotton spinning was introduced in the organized sector. This was the period when production of yarn was shifted from professional skills of the individuals to mechanical machines. Some textile units were established in Maharashtra and Gujarat. Although it was considered as a threat to the manual workers engaged in spinning of yarn, yet, this industry had a steady growth. This growth was further accelerated after 1950 and today textile industry contributes to 25 per cent of industrial production.

The cotton economy of India has witnessed a revolution that has gone virtually unsung and unheralded. Overcoming long periods of chronic short supply due to low level of harvest, accompanied by considerable instability from year to year, we have now achieved a qualitative and quantitative breakthrough. Production is well above the 100 lakh bale mark and embraces a wide range of varieties with spinning values from 2 counts to 120 counts a feat no other country can match. Because of this transition King cotton reigns supreme in our textile industry and production of yarn has increased by leaps and bounds and cotton yarn has emerged as a major foreign exchange earner. The fortunes of spinning mills are also looking up with both, the number of spindles installed and also the order of their utilization showing a very encouraging trend in recent years.

The Textiles and Clothing Industry is undergoing rapid restructuring globally and in India. Being labour intensive, the industry is showing shift from industrialized countries to developing countries. As a result global trade in Textiles and Clothing is increasing at a fast pace. The global trade in Textile and Clothing was placed at $ 350 billion in 1997, the Indian share being $ 10 billion (2.8%).

In India, the Textile Industry contributes 7% of the GDP and 17% of the value added in the manufacturing sector. It is the largest employer of industrial work force totaling 27 million workers. The Textile Industry is the single largest foreign exchange earner accounting for 32% share in the country's exports amounting to over Rs. 35,000 crores. The exports have been growing at over 20% for the last 5 years. The industry has significant advantage in terms of the availability of wide variety of cotton, low cost labour and a large domestic market. The export potential of Clothing and Textile Industry alone is estimated by various experts from $ 25 billion to $ 40 billion by 2010.

The Spinning Sector: The Textiles Industry ion India has experienced progressive disintegration with the composite mills giving way to independent spinners, weavers, knitters and garment makers. The spinning sector has grown to prominence with world's second largest capacity and employing modern technology. A significant trend is mushrooming of large number of EOUs in the spinning sector.

Weaving Sector: In weaving, the number of power looms has increased by leaps and bounds. There are estimated 14 lakh power looms operating in the country. The number of shuttles looms is placed at 8000. The powerloom sector claims a share of 70% in the country's total cloth production.

Knitting Sector: The knitting sector has recorded an impressive growth in the last ten years. There are about 50000 hosiery and knitting machines operating in the country producing about 13% of the total cloth production. This sector is likely to show the highest growth both in terms of quantity and value addition. A schematic presentation of the Textile industry is shown in Figure 1.

Figure – 1

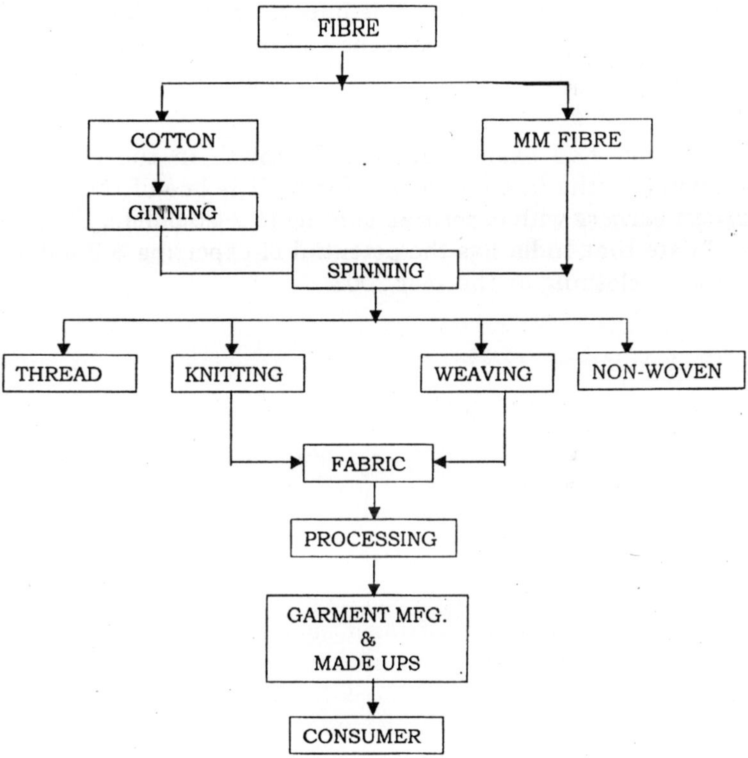

FIBRE
COTTON
MM FIBRE
GINNING
SPINNING
THREAD
KNITTING
WEAVING
NON-WOVEN
FABRIC
PROCESSING
GARMENT MFG. & MADE UPS
CONSUMER

Schematic presentation of the textile industry

Source: PSIDC Seminar on Textiles, 1998

CLOTHING

The Textile industry in India occupies a vital place in the country's economy and contributes substantially to export earnings. Garments make up nearly 16.8 per cent of the total textile exports. It is also a matter of pride for the garment export industry to be the highest net foreign exchange earner for the country.

With the developments, which are taking place in the international trade with the emerging of trading blocs and the disintegration of MFA within a decade, the garment industry will have to adapt itself so that the prominent position that it has in Indian economy continues to be maintained. In this context it is imperative that the industry diversifies its production and instead of being dominated by cotton Fibre, is able to use other type of fabrics in the synthetic area.

There has been phenomenal growth in the clothing Industry in the last ten years. Today, it is one of the major export earners with exports amounting to $ 4.5 billion. Experts estimate that India has the potential of exporting $ 9 billion worth of clothing by the year 2002.

4

The Doha Agenda and the Uruguay Round

INTRODUCTION

At the World Trade Organisation (WTO) Doha Ministerial Conference of November 2001 Trade Ministers agreed to open a new round of multilateral negotiations. Viewed from a development perspective the strength of the Doha outcome is the persistence of its commitment to helping developing countries. It provides however little perception of how to do so. My objective is to help to develop such a perception: to inform the development community of the Doha Agenda and to begin a dialogue on how the development community might help to turn the Agenda's commitment to development into action. To do so I review the outcome of the Uruguay Round, then apply the lessons I draw from this review to the Doha Agenda.

The Uruguay Round provides particularly relevant experience in that the Doha Agenda proposes to extend negotiations on many topics taken up in that Round. Furthermore, a major new concern about the WTO and development, "the implementation problem," stems from the Uruguay Round results.

It is important to note that only part of the Uruguay Round results has created an implementation problem. On tariff reductions, developing countries' commitments were larger than those of developed countries and all were fully implemented by the January 2000 deadline. Services trade is another area where developing countries made substantial commitments – though less here than developed countries – and there is no implementation problem. The approach I take is to compare where there is a Uruguay Round implementation problem for developing countries and where there is not. The immediate purpose of this analysis is to suggest how the negotiations might advance the development dimensions of the Doha Agenda, both where implementation has proceeded smoothly and where it has not.

The more ambitious purpose of the comparison is to provide a way of thinking about which development issues can be effectively addressed through WTO negotiations and which are more effectively addressed through development institutions such as the Asian Development Bank. WTO negotiations and development banks are different – created to address different issues, their evolutions conditioned by different objectives and constraints. What then is the "comparative advantage" of these different institutions, and what does an understanding of such comparative advantage suggest the role of each should be in advancing the various issues listed in the Doha Agenda?

This overview provides the basis to argue development institutions should take an active role in much of the Doha Agenda. On traditional trade liberalization they have a lot to offer, in the new areas they are indispensable.

The analysis of the Uruguay Round outcome deals with four basic propositions:

(i) The General Agreement on Tariffs and Trade (GATT) never evolved a capacity for project design or cost-benefit analysis because none was needed. With tariff reductions, legal obligation and project design are identical. Furthermore, what trade negotiators describe as a "concession" is, in real economics, a benefit for the giver as well as for the receiver. No need for cost-benefit analysis, a "diplomats' economics" is good enough.[1]

(ii) The new areas demand better economics. The new areas (services, standards, intellectual property) deal with behind-the-border regulations and

institutions that establish the fundamental structure of the domestic economy. There is a wide span between what is possible to write as generic obligation and what is needed *country-by-country* to develop functioning economic regulations and institutions and *the commercial capacities* to take advantage of them.

(iii) WTO negotiations (at least in rhetoric) limit themselves to the "trade-related aspects" of the new areas. Development however is about the nontrade-related aspects as well, about the environment in which domestic economic activity takes place. Often it is not possible to find the development dimensions of the new areas from their "trade-related aspects" much less to advance them.

(iv) Implementation in the new areas requires real investments: to provide laboratories, equipment, etc. This will take money and development expertise, of which trade ministers have neither

The remainder of the paper proceeds as follows. Section I provides a review of the Uruguay Round negotiations from the point of view of what the Round achieved in the areas of trade in goods and services as well as in the new areas of intellectual property and standards. Section II elaborates on the difference between the administrative burden of traditional tariff cuts and these new areas while Section III discusses these two new areas in more depth. Section IV discusses the Doha Agenda with particular reference to the challenges presented by the agenda items of market access, trade in services, intellectual property, standards, anti-dumping, and the so-called Singapore issues of competition policy, trade facilitation, and government procurement. The paper concludes with a series of recommendations in Section V.

1. URUGUAY ROUND OUTCOME

Few would question that opportunities offered by the open international trading system have been an important vehicle for development, nor that multilateral negotiations have played a critical role in creating that system. The Uruguay Round was a significant step, particularly in bringing developing countries to use multilateral negotiations as a vehicle for their own trade reforms.

A. Market Access Outcome and Impact

Much was achieved at the Uruguay Round:

(i) tariff cuts compared well to the coverage and depth of cuts achieved at the Tokyo and Kennedy Rounds;

(ii) agricultural protection was dealt with substantively for the first time;

(iii) quantitative restrictions on imports of textiles and clothing sanctioned under the Multi Fiber Arrangement (MFA) will be eliminated according to a schedule that extends until 2005;

(iv) developing countries agreed to tariff cuts even deeper than those agreed by developed countries, to bind nearly the same percentage of their tariffs as developed countries have bound.[2]

For the world in total, these liberalizations allowed an increase of some $75 billion per year of economic output from the same resource base – this figure, based on the size and price level of the world economy in 1992, is what economists would call the welfare gain.[3]

Figure 1 provides an indication of how this gain was distributed among economies. The chart shows that among regions of the world, Asian economies came out well though there are considerable differences from economy to economy.

While the mercantilist economics of trade negotiations often describes "own concessions" as a burden, in real economics a country will benefit from its own liberalization as well as from liberalization by its trading partners. Martin and Winters (1996, 13-14) provide evidence that countries that made the larger "concessions" at the Uruguay Round were the ones who gathered the larger benefits.[4]

Figure 2 presents information on a part of the trade liberalization outcome of particular interest to developing

Figure—1 Welfare Gains from Uruguay Round Liberalization

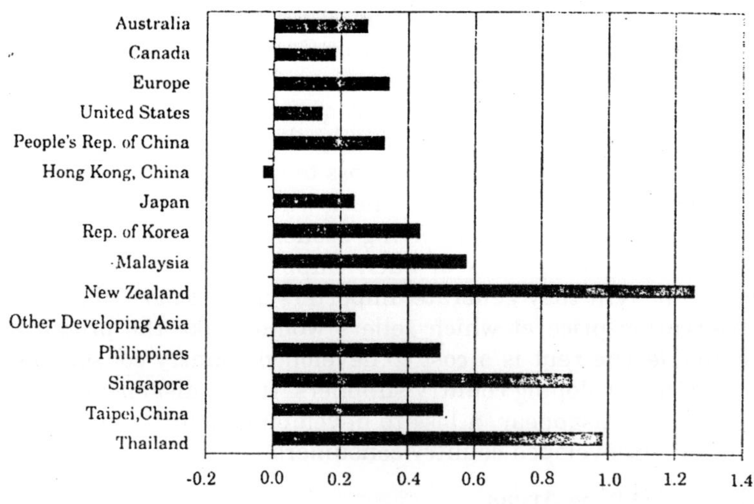

Source: Brown et. al (2001. Table 1).

Figure—2 Gain or Loss from Uruguay Round Elimination of MFA Quotas

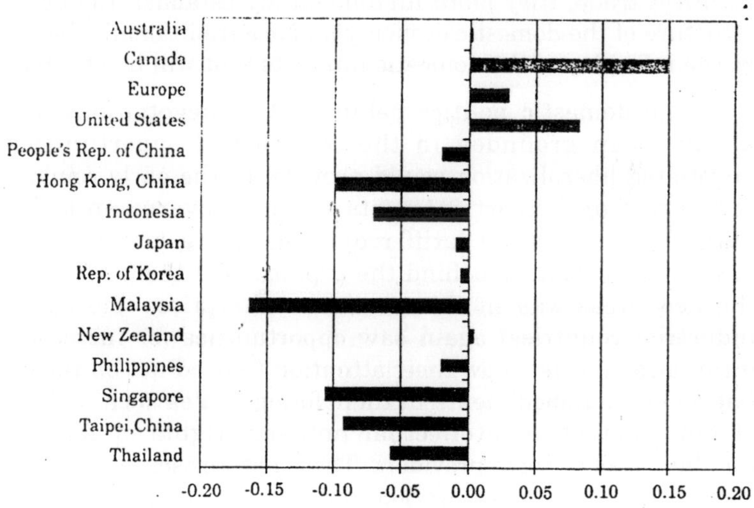

Source: Brown et. al (2001. Table 1).

economies, the impact of elimination of MFA sanctioned quotas on developed country imports of textiles and clothing. In negotiations such liberalization is typically viewed as a victory for exporters. But estimates of the economic impact indicates that elimination of MFA quotas will be a net benefit to the importing countries such as Canada and the United States as shown in the figure, a loss to many Asian developing countries who are exporters. There will be efficiency benefits to both exporting and importing economies, but a significant part of the economics of such import restrictions is the economic rent they generate: importers paying more than the reservation price at which sellers would make the products available.The rent is a cost to developed country consumers, a gain to developing country suppliers. It will disappear when the quotas disappear, a loss to developing country suppliers, a gain for developed country consumers.

B. WTO New Areas

Intellectual property rights, sanitary and industrial standards, and services are the principal WTO "New Areas." Regulations and institutions here are often described as "behind-the-border." Though the regulations and institutions do affect trade, they more fundamentally establish the basic structure of the domestic economy and are traditionally forged in the interplay of the domestic interests that will be affected.

The domestic politics behind GATT negotiations has always been grounded in the commercial opportunities negotiated liberalization would provide. In the early rounds, pressure from export interests to give governments the authority to negotiate tariff reductions was a key element. The domestic politics behind the expansion of the GATT into the new areas was similar. Business enterprises (mostly in industrial countries) again saw opportunities for increased international sales; now their attention focused not on tariffs but on other impediments to their foreign sales such as lack of enforcement of intellectual property rights or foreign regulations of services providers. These enterprises, along with their trade negotiators, worked out ways to use GATT/WTO mechanisms to bring pressure on foreign governments to make such changes.[5]

C. Different Agreements Provide Opportunities in Different Ways

The various New Areas agreements work in different ways. GATS, the General Agreement on Trade in Services, provides a conceptual framework for negotiating cross-border commercial opportunities, e.g., opportunities for foreign companies to set up offices. The agreement however applies a minimum of generic obligations. As with tariffs, obligations here are given legal meaning as schedules of specific commitments attached to the agreement. The commitments might be (i) general, e.g.., giving foreign-licensed accountants the opportunity to operate within the country on the same basis as domestically licensed ones; or (ii) more guarded, e.g., giving foreign companies the opportunity to establish retail stores, but limited to no more than 1,500 square meters of floor space and not more than one store per city.

TRIPS, the Agreement on Trade-Related Aspects of Intellectual Property Rights, does introduce generic obligations—minimum standards for legal recognition of intellectual property rights and for enforcement of these rights of holders—on foreigners and nationals. The TRIPS agreement incorporates and sometimes extends standards expressed in relevant international conventions such as the Paris Convention for the Protection of Industrial Property (for patents) and parallel international conventions on copyright, trademarks, trade secrets, industrial designs and layout designs of integrated circuits. The standards imposed are more or less the highest in place among developed Members when the agreement was negotiated, in some cases even higher than that (Reichman 1998).

There are two standards agreements, one on industrial standards, another on sanitary and phyto-sanitary standards (SPS). They are structured to give exporters a basis for complaining about the use of standards as disguised import protection. If an exporting Member suspects that a standard is being applied to restrict imports rather than to ensure safety or quality, the Member can challenge application of the standard. If the standard is one recognized by the relevant international convention (e.g., the Codex Alimentarius for food safety) the exporter's burden is to demonstrate that the standard has been misapplied. If the standard in question is different from an internationally recognized one, then the (importer) government applying it has the burden to prove that the standard and its application are in fact based on science and applied equally to domestic and foreign products. In effect, standards recognized by international conventions are presumed consistent with the WTO agreements; other standards bear the burden of proof. As with intellectual property, this makes standards and systems already in place in developed countries more or less the norm, leaving the implementation burden mostly on developing countries.

D. Implementation Successes and Problems in Developing Countries

In the Uruguay Round negotiations on market access, developing countries were active participants and committed themselves to extensive reforms that were as broad in scope and deeper than those of developed countries. Implementation here met the 1 January 2000 deadline without complaint. It went smoothly because developing country governments were confident of their capacity to manage economic policy in the areas affected by their commitments. Many had a decade or more of unilateral liberalization to build on. The interests that would be affected comprehended the benefits from such policy changes; the government was familiar with managing the trade offs between domestic winners and losers.

The services negotiations provide another example of successful implementation. Many economic reform programmes that took place in developing countries in the 1980s and 1990s included liberalization of the services sector. In many cases reform included a decision to bind foreign access and national treatment at the WTO (Finger and Nogués 2001). (Table 1 compares the extent of commitment between developing and developed countries in selected areas.) In developing countries as in developed, the domestic politics of these reforms was built on domestic considerations rather than on the clout of international obligation. While in developed countries reform decisions were largely motivated by the opportunities businesses saw for increased foreign revenues, in developing countries they were brought about by user complaints about the quality of services available (Finger and Nogués 2001).

Table—1 Uruguay Round Outcome: Percentages of Developing and of Developed Economies that Made Some Market Access or Some National Treatment Commitments on Selected Service Sectors

Cross Border Provision	*Market Access*		*National Treatment*	
	Developing Economies	*Developed Economies*	*Developing Economies*	*Developed Economies*
Professional services	22	71	22	71
Communication services	37	97	36	97
Distribution services	12	96	12	96
Financial services	26	37	26	37
All selected sectors	25	70	25	70
Commercial Presence	*Market Access*		*National Treatment*	
	Developing Economies	*Developed Economies*	*Developing Economies*	*Developed Economies*
Professional services	22	71	22	71
Communication services	37	97	36	97
Distribution services	18	96	18	96
Financial services	47	98	46	98
All selected sectors	36	94	35	95

Sources: Finger and Schuknecht (2001, Table S4).

Most of the complaints about developing country implementation relate to the intellectual property and the standards agreements. An important difference between these agreements and the market access and services agreements is that the standards and intellectual property agreements impose generic obligations. Differences between the economics of such generic New Areas obligations vs. traditional market access obligations are taken up in the following section.

II. TRADE LIBERALIZATION AND NEW AREAS: REFORMS HAVE DIFFERENT ECONOMICS

The administrative part of tariff cuts is easy. Reaching agreement demands considerable diplomatic skill. Squaring the agreement to cut tariffs with domestic politics requires considerable political courage, but tariff reforms agreed in a multilateral negotiation can be implemented with the stroke of a minister's or a legislature's pen. New lists of tariff rates are posted, and customs agents apply those rates rather than the previous ones. Furthermore, the economics is foolproof. Though mercantilist economics considers a tariff reduction a "concession", in real economics *giving* such a concession is something that *adds to* the national economic interest—the real economics of a concession is positive for the giver as well as for the receiver. GATT bargaining, remember, is a response to the difficult politics of liberalization, not to the good sense of its economics.

A. Implementation has a Real Cost

The economics of new areas commitments differs in several ways. For one, implementing new areas obligations will require real resources. Where laws must be revised and enforcement agencies buttressed or created, expensive legal expertise is needed. Where obligations involve standards, laboratories, equipment, and scientifically trained personnel are necessary. All in all, World Bank project experience indicates that it will cost a developing country $150 million to get pup to speed in only three of the New Areas: intellectual property rights, SPS, and customs valuation. This $150 million is more than a full year's development budget in many of the least developed countries (Finger and Schuler 2000).

B. Implementation can be Bad Economics

Perhaps more significant, development experience as revealed by World Bank-supported projects indicates that the money might be ill-spent. WTO agreements provide sometimes an incorrect diagnosis of and sometimes an inappropriate remedy for the problems developing countries face. For example, the customs agreement covers only valuation, but project experience in developing countries indicates that valuation is perhaps the last centimeter in a whole meter of customs processes that requires reform. Developing country projects here deal with more basic issues of physical security, objectivity, and accountability—determination against an explicit standard rather than through informal negotiation with customs officials Fitting the WTO-required valuation accounting into present customs systems would likely increase, rather than reduce, the opportunities for a negotiated, as opposed to an objective, outcome (Finger 2001).

More striking still, through TRIPS developing countries took on as legal obligation a cost of $60 billion per year, but there is no legal obligation in the agreement on any Member to provide anything in exchange. This point will be taken up in Section III below.

C. Development Institutions not Trade Negotiations are Designed to Take on Such Economics

Generally speaking, tools that serve well in one use may not serve well in another. It is possible that the "comparative advantage" of multilateral negotiations to support correct policy choices on trade restrictions does not carry over to the construction of behind-the-border regulations and institutions that provide the basic business environment.

On trade restrictions, each country has the sovereign authority to impose them and most tend to overdo it. The advantage of concentrated producer interests over disbursed consumer interests is the familiar explanation—the political incorrectness of unilateral openness dominates its economic correctness.

Reducing import restrictions though reciprocal exchange alters the politics. For one thing, it brings not only export interests into the game, it brings in general foreign policy interests to support liberalization. In the years just after World War II the view that a web of countries interlinked by commerce would contribute to peace and security was an important part of the base for negotiations. Taking up import liberalization through multilateral negotiations did little to change the mercantilist perception that imports were the costs of trade, instead, it shifted attention to other effects that the public considered more important.

To the negotiators the GATT process was diplomacy, not economics. There was a casual concern that each country accept more or less the same depth of cut on more or less the same fraction of imports, but no delegation equipped itself with precise tabulations of either its own or its trading partners' concessions—much less with analysis of the effects of such on trade, production, or economic welfare. Furthermore, GATT's "member countries" saw no need to create a Secretariat capacity for such tabulation or analysis.[6]

As an instrument to help the international community make correct decisions about the reduction of trade barriers, multilateral negotiations did not need a capacity for economic analysis. What in mercantilist economics is a "concession" is in real economics a benefit to the concession *giver* as well as to the concession *receiver*. The economic results are positive for all parties.[7] Furthermore, implementation requires no investment. While the politics of reaching agreement might be difficult, implementing the lower tariff rates requires no more than an official document instructing customs agents accordingly.

Development institutions were created to take on different issues with more difficult economics. To create or replace a transport system or an education system is different from reaching an agreement to mutually reduce import restrictions in two key ways: it requires real investment, and it brings one into the realm where some alternatives have higher rates of return than others. These matters require a different set of tools, one that includes project design and cost-benefit analysis.

Legal obligation is a familiar GATT/WTO tool; perhaps less recognized is that development institutions also employ legal obligations. Differences in the tasks of GATT/WTO and of development institutions have led to different forms of legal obligation. With a development institution, a country's legal obligations are the commitments it makes when it borrows money from the institution. One country may borrow to finance transportation, another to finance education; within education one country may need classrooms, another teachers. Hence with a development institutions are more suited to the one-off problems and trial-error rhythm of what is needed to build behind-the-border regulations and institutions for countries at different levels of development than is WTO's generic approach to legal obligation.

With negotiations, legal obligation comes before project design and cost-benefit analysis; with development institutions it comes after. When the objective was reduction of import restrictions, this difference did not matter. When the objective is to set up behind-the-border regulations and institutions, it does matter. The following section elaborates.

III. LESSONS FROM TRIPS AND STANDARDS

The TRIPS agreement for intellectual property rights obligates member governments to provide the regulations and the enforcement mechanism that would allow owners of intellectual property to establish and defend these rights—i.e. to collect revenues on them in all Member countries. More simply, it has the effect of creating claims by intellectual property owners against intellectual property users. As developing countries are more often users than vendors of intellectual property, the impact is a significant economic obligation on developing countries – users owe royalties, copyright fees, etc. on the use of knowledge not previously protected in their countries by patents, copyrights, etc. As with the economics of the MFA, these are basically economic rents: negative in adding up the gross domestic product(GDP) of those who pay, positive in the GDP of those who receive.

A. Magnitude of the TRIPS Obligation

The world Bank provides estimates of one part of that obligation, the obligation created by increased patent claims by owners of intellectual property (World Bank 2002). Table 2 reports estimates of the amounts by which full implementation of TRIPS obligations on patents would change net payments. For the first six countries on the list (United States, Germany, Japan, France, United Kingdom, and Switzerland), the figures sum to $40 billion/year of increased payments.

Table—2 Change of Net Annual Patent Rent Obligations Resulting from Full Application of TRIPS (millions of 2000 dollars)

Country	*Net Change of Patent Rents*
United States	19,083
Germany	6,768
Japan	5,673
France	3,326
United Kingdom	2,968
Switzerland	2,000
Australia	1,097
Netherlands	241
Ireland	18
Portugal	–282
Canada	–574
New Zealand	–2,204
Spain	–4,716
Greece	–7,746
South Africa	–11
Brazil	–530
India	–903
Mexico	–2,550
Israel	–3,894
People's Rep. of China	–5,121
Rep. of Korea	–15,333

Source: World Bank (2002, Table 5.1).

The International Intellectual Property Alliance's (IIPA) estimates of losses from copyright piracy provide additional information on the obligation implicit in the TRIPS agreement.[8] IIPA estimates that losses due to piracy of US (alone) copyrighted material around the world at some $20-22 billion per year (IIPA 2002a).

B. The Quid Pro Quo

The Uruguay Round "grand bargain" was that developing countries would take on obligations in the new areas and in exchange developed countries would provide better access to their markets, particularly on agricultural products and on textiles and clothing.

As compared with the outcome of the market access negotiations, the TRIPS amounts described above are big money. Comparing (Table 3) the net gains from changed patent obligations with the gains from Uruguay Round liberalization of tariffs on industrial goods by *all* WTO Members shows that TRIPS-patents are worth *13 times* more to the US than is the Uruguay Round tariff package on

Table—3. TRIPS Patent Requirements and Uruguay Round Tariff Liberalization on Industrial Goods: Impacts Compared

Country	*Gain from TRIPS Patents Requirements / Gain from Industrial Goods Tariff Liberalization (ratio, not percentage)*
United States	13.1
Germany + France+ United Kingdom#	3.6
Japan	2.1
Australia	1.8
People's Rep. of China	–4.7
Mexico	–7.0
Rep. of Korea	–18.0

Note: # The line for Germany + France + United Kingdom compares the gains from TRIPS-patents requirements for these three countries with Harrison et. at estimates of the gains from tariff liberalization to all members of the European Union.

Sources: Estimates of TRIPS impact: World Bank (2002, Table 5.1). Impact of tariff liberalization on industrial goods: Harrison et. al (1996, Table 8.6).

industrial goods. On the other side of the ledger, for the three developing countries for which both the World Bank and the Harrison et. al estimates are available, TRIPS-patents bring increased claims *against* them several times larger than what they will gain from Uruguay Round tariff liberalization on industrial goods. For Republic of Korea, the TRIPS obligation is 18 times as large as her gain. Table 4 likewise compares the IIPA estimates of copyright obligations with gains from Uruguay Round tariff liberalization on industrial goods. Again, data from the two sources overlap for only a few Members. Of these, only in the case of Argentina is the ratio greater than one, i.e., copyright obligations greater than gains from trade liberalization.

Table—4 IIPA Copyright Obligation Estimates and Uruguay Round Tariff Liberalization on Industrial Goods: Impacts Compared

Member	*Copyright Obligation / Gain from Industrial Goods Tariff Liberalization (ratio, not percentage)*
Argentina	1.22
People's Rep. of China	0.97
Taipei, China	0.53
Brazil	0.49
Indonesia	0.19
Malaysia	0.16
Thailand	0.12

Sources: Impact of copyright obligations: IIPA (2002b). Impact of tariff liberalization on industrial goods: Harrison et. al (1996, Table 8.6).

Taking into account agricultural plus textiles and clothing liberalization would not make the comparison look more favourable for developing countries. As noted in Section I, agricultural liberalization was minimal; removal of import quotas on textiles and clothing is a loss for developing countries, a gain for developed.

There is a plausible economic argument that the higher level of intellectual property protection the TRIPS agreement demands will attract foreign investment into developing countries, and induce inventions particularly suited to the needs and opportunities of the developing countries. Conversely, one might argue that once the intellectual property rights of outsiders are recognized there is less need for a local presence, and that the opportunity to produce unlicensed copies free from legal hassle may be the more attractive investment opportunity. The evidence here is mixed,[9] but whichever way it cuts it imposes no legally bound obligation. A Member cannot take "economists", much less "investors" or "inventors" before the WTO dispute settlement body if no investment or invention results. The New Area agreements also promise technical assistance for implementation, but these promises avoid the compulsion of legal obligation. They are unbound promises that developing countries accepted pin exchange for their legally binding obligation to pay $60 billion per year.

C. A Legal Obligation is not an Economic Result

The numbers presented above – that cover only patents and copyrights for a few countries—sum to a claim of $60 billion/year. However, having a claim on $60 billion/year and collecting it are not the same. In between the two lie both the mechanics of collection and the "wiggle room" in the TRIPS text, or more diplomatically phrased, the "creative ambiguity" on which the magnitude of the claim might be questioned.

Available facts suggest that there is considerable slippage from claim to collection—owners of these claims sometimes settle for a few cents on the dollar. Bristol-Myers, the New York Times reported, has offered to sell in Africa a leading AIDS medicine at $1 for a day's dosage; the price in the US is $18 (Petersen and McNeil 2001). IIPA data report low collection rates in many countries on copyrighted products; e.g., on copyrighted business software, collection rates of less than 50 per cent in more than three quarters of the 39 countries covered by a recent survey; collection rates on entertainment software of less than 10 per cent in many countries.

D. Converting Claims into Commercial Realities is Business, not Diplomacy

In the US, the affected business interests are at the front line to spot commercial opportunities to which other countries' WTO obligations might give them claim and to identify changes of foreign regulations and enforcement practices that would enable them to increase their revenues. This information and the people who assemble it are linked to US negotiators through a formal, legally established Industry Consultations Programme that advises on trade negotiations and on the system the US Congress has established to support US enterprises to advance their commercial interests abroad. "Section 301" and "Special 301" are familiar instruments created to implement these interests.[10]

The Industry Consultations Programme and its related business associations play a similar role in developing US negotiating agendas and in evaluating proposals from others. The system provides a business perspective that evaluates the potential revenue from different trade-related activities for a variety of business interests. It also provides an advantage in the depth of expertise the US brings to WTO negotiations that is perhaps as important as the larger scope of expertise that has been documented by comparing sizes of Geneva delegations (Michalopolous 1999). The system provides constituent ownership of the US negotiating position.

Trade policy in the US is *business*. Having and bringing to bear the business/legal skill to *capitalize* the outcome is critical, not just after the agreement is in place, but to negotiate it in the first place.

E. Apples for Oranges: It Never Did Work

It is important to notice how different is the exchange implicit in agreements that function by establishing a common standard versus those that are a direct exchange of concessions. Such is exemplified by the differences between tariff negotiations and TRIPS. However it is equally important to notice that the difference is not between traditional market access and new areas. GATS, through its process of specific, scheduled negotiations, has the capacity to avoid the problems taken up in this section.

1. *All Reciprocity is Local*[11]

Trade negotiations have never supported broad exchanges. Even within tariff negotiations, exchanges that demanded significant shifts across sectors have been difficult; agriculture, textiles and clothing have been handled separately from the normal exchange of concessions. The problem with shifts across sectors is to achieve *domestic* reciprocity; e.g., paying the US textile industry from gains enjoyed by the US aircraft industry. There have been few such direct swaps. Overcoming resistance from potential losers has been, in practice, part power politics, e.g., where negotiating authority must be specifically granted, using export industries to win more Congressional votes than the opposition could rally. It has been, in other part, compensation. Adjustment assistance is the straight forward example, the familiar political coin of public works has also been used.[12]

With agriculture and textiles and clothing set aside, much of the growth of trade has been intra-industry. Gilbert Winham reports (1986, 65) a tendency to look for "self-balancing sectors"—or, one might add, to construct them; e.g. craft North American Free Trade Agreement rules of origin to condition access to the US market for textile products on the use of US-made fibers or fabrics.

2. *Shifting Among Constituencies Versus Creating Constituencies*

Tariff negotiations worked by switching domestic political clout from one producer constituency to another, from import competing industries to exporters. The politics was relatively easy because the receiving constituency already existed and it was more dynamic than the one who lost influence.

Taking up intellectual property rights as a trade issue cannot build on a similar shift within domestic politics (in poorer countries there is no producer constituency for intellectual property rights) perhaps because these economies have come to depend on knowledge from outside. The easier politics of shifting domestic political support to an existing (and dynamic) constituency is not available.[13] For intellectual property rights to take root, a constituency to support the reform that the agreement demands must be built.

3. *Domestic Reciprocity is the Challenge*

In summary, exchanging market access for intellectual property rights brings with it a more challenging domestic politics than do more traditional trade agreements. It demands a broader domestic pay-off from winners to losers than trade negotiations have supported in the past. It also requires that the benefiting domestic constituency be *created* by the exchange, something trade negotiations have never done. The advantage the advanced countries have to let their commercial constituencies lead the negotiations (to depend on them to identify possible benefits and risks) may be insurmountable. The complementary constituencies do not exist in most developing countries.

4. *This is What Development Institutions Do, Not Trade Negotiations*

With tariff concessions, project design follows directly and obviously from legal obligation. A commitment to lower tariffs brings forward minimal issues of "How"? The same is not true for intellectual property, standards, and other behind-the-border areas of regulation and institutions. A commitment to enforce intellectual property rights is a long way from a judicial and legal enforcement system that will do so. Here there is a broad gap between project design and the generalities that a generic, one-size-fits-all, statement of legal obligation can provide. There is also a considerable need for cost-benefit analysis, as a considerable share of the development budget may be at stake, rate of return comparisons are a necessary part of good management. Development institutions will have to lead here, trade negotiations cannot.

IV. THE DOHA AGENDA: SUMMARY AND COMMENTARY

The Appendix summarizes the content of the work programme that the Doha Ministerial Declaration sets out.

There are three categories: (i) subjects on which there will be negotiations,[14] (ii) subjects on which negotiations will not be opened though there will be continuing WTO work within special working groups, and (iii) cross-cutting considerations related mostly to how development or developing countries will be included in the negotiations.

This section expands on the summary given in the Appendix. It applies the lessons drawn from the previous discussion to a selected number of negotiating issues. The purpose of this section is to provide an overview and to initiate a discussion of the Doha Agenda from a development perspective.

A. Market Access: Import Restrictions on Agricultural and Non-agricultual Products

The removal of distortions to agricultural trade and of import restrictions on industrial goods is the trade agenda most directly linked to poverty reduction and economic development. Agriculture is important because poverty in developing countries is in large part rural. Industrial reform is important because many poor people work in the production of basic manufactures. Getting rid of developing country restrictions is as important as getting rid of developed country restrictions. Developing countries are a large market. Their protection is as biased against the exports of developing countries—and considerably higher—than is developed country protection.

On agriculture the Doha Declaration lists import protection, export subsidies, and domestic support as subjects for negotiation. However, it also expressly acknowledges the possibility of accomplishing nothing—"without prejudging the outcome of the negotiation" is the phrase. It goes on to explicitly recognize the domestic politics in developed and in developing counties of doing nothing. It also commits to making operational the absence of reform commitment by developing countries. One finds little there to indicate a momentum toward reform.

On non-agricultural products the declaration names tariff peaks, tariff escalation, and products of export interest to developing countries as specific targets. These are important targets.

The Declaration also commits to "take full into account the special needs and interests of developing and least developed country participants, including through less than full reciprocity in reduction commitments." The comparable statement in the Punta del Este Declaration (that launched the Uruguay Round) pointed in the opposite direction, saying "Emphasis shall be given the expansion of the scope of tariff concessions among all participants."

If this shift represents backing off good economics in order to win agreement to hold negotiations, then its priorities are wrong; likewise if it represents backing away from developing country trade liberalization on merchandise in order to maintain pressure on New Areas implementation. It the shift bought the inclusion of the Singapore issues (discussed below) then the priorities are particularly wrong.

B. Services

As discussed above (Section I.D) the services agreement has proved to be a useful vehicle for solidifying reforms in developing countries. The agreement—a framework for negotiation of one-by-one liberalizations—is more suited to the realities of the underlying economics and particularly to the underlying politics than are other "new areas" agreements. The politics is largely domestic, as the interests of users, particularly of producers who need business services of competitive quality at competitive prices are served by services liberalization. (Table 5 provides information of the share of services in the imports and the exports of Asian countries). The Doha Declaration paragraph carries forward without qualification the basis for previously successful negotiations.

C. Trade-Related Aspects in Intellectual Property Rights

On intellectual property, the Ministerial declaration narrowly constrains the negotiating agenda to geographic indicators, and within that subject to a multilateral system of notification and registration for such. Possible extension of protection of geographic indicators is left to an inquiry by the

TRIPS Council, which is also to look into the relation between TRIPS and the Convention on Biological Diversity, and into the protection of traditional knowledge and folklore.

The Doha Ministerial also produced a separate Declaration on TRIPS and public health, worded ambiguously enough so that one side could say that existing legal obligations were maintained, the other that their position on the overriding importance of public health over individual owners' rights had been vindicated. In a legal sense, there has been no agreement to renegotiate TRIPS. In a commercial sense TRIPS is being renegotiated every day. The one dollar in eighteen offer on AIDS pharmaceuticals is one illustration. The bilateral negotiations over how far a country must advance to protect the interests of US owners of intellectual property in order to maintain or regain eligibility for US tariff preferences are another example. The US Trade representative's "watch list" indicates that such negotiations are under way with some 50 countries.

Table—5: Services Trade as a Percentage of Merchandise trade, 1999

	Export+Imports: Commercial Services As % of Merchandise	*Exports: Commercial Services as % of Merchandise*	*Imports: Commercial Services as % of Merchandise*
1	**2**	**3**	**4**
World	23	23	23
North America	22	30	17
Latin America	19	18	19
Western Europe	26	27	25
Africa	27	27	28
Asia	21	18	25
Australia	28	30	26
Japan	24	14	37
New Zealand	33	34	31
Australia+Japan+NewZealand	25	17	35

(Contd...)

1	2	3	4
Other Asia	36	32	39
Bangladesh	12	5	17
Combodia	29	21	36
PRC	16	13	19
Fiji	61	78	48
Hong Kong, China	122	166	89
India	38	38	38
Indonesia	22	9	47
Korea, Rep. of	20	18	22
Lao PDR	18	32	9
Macao, China	78	123	29
Malaysia	18	14	23
Maldives	98	548	27
Mangolia	28	22	33
Myanmar	21	38	12
Nepal	25	50	14
Pakistan	19	17	20
Papua New Guinea	32	13	61
Philippines	18	13	23
Samoa	49	235	17
Singapore	32	34	29
Soloman Islands	54	35	78
Sri Lanka	22	20	23
Taipei, China	17	14	21
Thailand	26	25	27
Vanuatu	126	408	50
Vietnam	27	24	31

Source: Tabulated from WTO data (available: http://www.wto.org/english/res_e/statis_e/its2001_e/appendix/a07.xls).

These often bilateral struggles over the claims on revenues that the TRIPS agreement establishes solidify the idea that one side has something to gain the other something to lose. They do nothing to develop an understanding of now and in what form intellectual property rights might contribute to development.

Several World Rank projects have been mounted to help poor people to earn more from their knowledge. In these projects the objective is commercial: increased earnings from knowledge. A revised legal structure is among the instruments that might help to advance this objective. In these projects, sometimes better patent or copyright enforcement is part of the solution, other times supply capacity, better marketing, getting rid of governmental red tape such as export controls or access to imported inputs and other directly commercial tools are more important. A tentative conclusion from this work is that when the objective is to help poor people earn more from their knowledge, TRIPS is neither an instrument nor impediment. Its wiggle room can accommodate things that work for poor people, its concepts do not help to find them.

An obvious reason to be skeptical that the "development dimension" of intellectual property rights will trickle down from TRIPS is that TRIPS, at least in law, deals only with the *trade-related* aspects of intellectual property rights. Its coverage of the development dimension is thus limited *to the development dimension of the trade-related aspects* of intellectual property. This leaves out a lost of people. In Senegal, for example, of some 30,000 musicians who complain about counterfeit reproductions and radio stations who play their music without paying royalties, less than 10 enjoy international sales. For the other 29,990, intellectual property rights is not trade-related, it is strictly a domestic issue. TRIPS provides no basis for the 29,990 to petition for better enforcement of copyright on their behalf.

Knowledge has an important role in development, and intellectual property rights have a role in turning knowledge into a commercial asset, in helping poor people to earn more from knowledge. Development institutions should lead here, trade negotiations cannot.

D. Singapore Issues

The basket many have labeled "Singapore Issues" contains investment, competition policy, transparency in government procurement, and trade facilitation. To investment and competition policy the Declaration attaches the familiar but hardly operational qualification, "trade-related aspects only." The government procurement negotiations—explicitly—will not take up restricting the scope for countries to give preferences to domestic supplies and suppliers.

On competition policy, Winters (2002) argues convincingly that an agreement—like other New Area agreement—would require (though not necessarily legally obligate) developing countries to adopt developed country practices and standards. If a developed and developing country were acting together against a hard-core cartel, Winters reasons, the developed country government would not want its case undermined by laxity on the part of the developing country. This, like other New Area obligations, would cost considerable money to establish and then to operate, which many developing countries could not afford. Winters (2002) points out that the Anti-Trust Division of the US Justice Department had a budget in 2000 of $110 million, the UK Office of fair Trading a staff of 450 and a budget of $33 million.

As with the standards agreements, an agreement on competition policy would not necessarily obligate a poor country to establish a competition authority that met such standards, but it would provide a basis for countries who already meet the standards to challenge actions by those who do not. Procurement obligations could have the same effect.

Investment negotiations and competition policy negotiations raise questions about the possibility of finding within the agreement a balance of concessions given versus concessions received. Again the thrust of the agreement would be toward imposing as international obligation the policies already in place in the developed countries. It might make economic sense for developing countries to do so, but such is a decision more effectively made through the processes of development institutions: country-specific evaluation of policy alternatives from the perspective of their costs and benefits. Bringing forward such reforms as concessions to foreign interests tends to focus on their costs and to underplay their benefits.

The concerns Finger and Schuler (2000) have raised about taking up the Uruguay Round New Area issues from the perspective of their trade-related aspects also apply to the Singapore issues. There are two issues. First such new regulations and institutions cost money to negotiate and to implement, money that might have a higher development pay-off somewhere else, e.g., in education for women. Second, their trade-related aspects as viewed by trading partners may be a poor guide to their economic development dimensions.

Finally, developing country concessions on Singapore issues could be a claim developed countries will press in order to counter pressure on them to make concessions in agriculture.

E. Antidumping

The Declaration paragraph on WTO rules specifies that there will be negotiations on antidumping; to clarify and to improve disciplines while preserving basic concepts.

The relevant concept from negotiating history is water in the tariff. When GATT began, tariffs where more than high enough to protect domestic suppliers—the first few rounds of GATT tariff negotiations then had little trade impact.

Though negotiations have moved tariffs from high to low, they have moved antidumping rules from simple to complex. There are today sufficient technicalities that any national authority of a mind to reach an affirmative determination can make a case. At the same time, any WTO panel so disposed will be able to find a technicality on which to discredit the national determination. (use of antidumping is burgeoning, so far every antidumping case brought to the WTO has been found inconsistent with the national authority's obligations.) Adding a few technicalities here, trimming a few there, will have no impact.[15]

In the initial GATT, trade remedies were a "pressure value", an instrument government used to manage domestic policies to maintain a policy of liberalization. As usage evolved, trade remedies have become expressions of the rights of import-competing interests to protection—an entitlement owned by import-competing industries that government must honour.

To return antidumping and other trade remedies to their original GATT perception will depend on changing first the domestic politics of trade remedies. This requires putting the interests of users of imports on the same basis as those of import-competing producers. It is not likely that international negotiations will do so; the entrenched antidumping users have an even tighter grip on the international negotiators than on the domestic policies of application.[16]

Developing countries have been since the Uruguay Round more frequent users of antidumping than developed countries.[17] This raises suspicion that on a WTO draft that really would provide discipline, developing country negotiators would not be able to deliver the agencies of their own governments that operate antidumping mechanisms.

F. Subsidies

The subsidies negotiations have more or less the same terms of reference as the antidumping negotiations—to clarify and to improve disciplines while preserving basic concepts. Fisheries subsidies will be on the table. Environmental interests and economic analysis both suggest removal of such subsidies.

The tendency in negotiations to defend one's own policies without regard to their economic impact is particularly dangerous here. To point out that the agriculture agreement, for example, allows developed countries to maintain larger subsidies than developing countries are allowed is a mercantilist debating point, it is not sound policy advice for developing countries. The development dimension must be found in sound analysis of what makes sense as domestic economic policy.

G. Technical Assistance, Capacity-Building

The topic of trade-related technical assistance or capacity building covers a wide range of possible activities. It might include, for example:

(i) reforming laws and regulations as WTO obligations demand;

(ii) providing the staff, staff training, laboratoties, computers, etc. to make the regulations work;

(iii) maintaining larger Geneva delegations, engaging more actively in WTO affairs;

(iv) improving developing countries' overall capacity to respond to the opportunities offered by the trading system.[18]

We know a little about that the first two of these would cost. An estimate for a small country of the cost of the requisite legal reforms is $10 million (English, Hoekman, and Mattoo 2002, Box 48.1). Add the equipment needed for a larger country with significant interests in agricultural exports and therefore considerable need for laboratory equipment, quarantine stations, etc. the figure comes to $150 million (Finger and Schuler 2000).

There has been considerable pressure for help through the WTO, but Trade Ministers and ministries do not have authority or even influence within their governments over the relevant sums. For 2002 the WTO budget for technical cooperation missions plus trade policy training courses totals 3,694,000 Swiss Francs, just over $2 million (WTO 2002a). The WTO has over 100 developing Members. Several WTO members have taken the initiative to organize a Doha Development Agenda Global Trust Fund, which has a target of 15 million Swiss Francs to support technical assistance and capacity-building (WTO 2002b).

The stalemate at the WTO over provision of such assistance has prompted Rubens Ricupero (2000) to suggest that in the future, negotiations over topics that will involve expensive implementation be accompanied by an "implementation audit." Such an audit would identify concretely what developing countries will have to do and what it will cost. Short of a bound commitment from the developed countries to meet such costs, statements about implementation assistance would be left out. This would avoid creating the rhetoric (only) of reciprocity by exchanging bound commitments for unbound promises.

H. Implementation

The Doha Declaration provides that where there that is a specific negotiating mandate implementation issues will be included in the negotiations. Other implementation issues will be addressed "as a matter of priority" by the relevant WTO bodies. The additional Doha Decision on Implementation-Related Issues and Concerns provides some insight into what the Ministers conceive as the content of "implementation." Table 6 provides a tabulation of the 45 individual points included in that Decision.

Table—6 Doha Decision on Implementation: Tabulation of Individual Points by Subject

Subject	*Number of Points*
Use or extension of special and differential Treatment provisions	16
Phase-in	10
Review to clarify certain part of the antidumping, subsidies, and TRIPS agreements	8
Technical assistance (unbound)	
To participate in the WTO or standards-related International bodies	4
To implement WTO obligations	6
Reminder that Members have a *legal obligation* Under TRIPS Acticle 66.2 to provide incentives for their enterprises and institutions to promote technology transfer to least developed countries	1

Note: This interpretation is intended to be explanatory but has no official standing. All questions about meaning of the Decision should refer to the text of the Decision.

The Decision introduces no new concepts on what might to done; all of the points fall into familiar GATT/WTO categories. They do not have much substance. Many of the Decision points "reaffirm", some ask for review, one "agrees that investigating authorities shall examine with special care." Sixteen are about special and differential treatment. The Ministers, for example, instruct the WTO Committee on Trade and Development to make a list of special and differential treatment provisions in the WTO agreements and to provide recommendations on ways in which they might be made more effective and on which of them might be made mandatory. Ten are about technical assistance, with no indication that the WTO Ministers have any more influence over the needed resources than they had when the Uruguay Round promises were made.

Perhaps the most substantive of the 45 points deals with a Uruguay Round subsidy agreement provision that allows a country with per capita income below $1,000/year to grant certain subsidies prohibited to other countries. The Ministers in the Decision take the matter further. They state agreement that if a Member's per capita income rises above $1000/year, then later falls below, the country again is clear to grant such subsidies.

V. Conclusions and Recommendations

Multilateral trade liberalization has been an indispensable part of development. It provides export opportunities, stimulus for domestic reforms, and discipline against domestic backsliding. Today the trade agenda most directly linked to poverty reduction and economic development is the removal of distortions to agricultural trade and of import restrictions on industrial goods.

To keep development moving, reducing developing country protection is as critical as reducing developed country protection. Active participation in multilateral liberalization is perhaps a more important part of developing country reform now than it was a decade ago. The groundwork for developing country participation in the Uruguay Round was the domestic politics underpinning several decades of unilateral reform. Active participation of the Uruguay Round increased the dependence of their domestic politics on outside pressure for continued reform. It is therefore even more important now than it was as the Uruguay Round to maintain pressure through the WTO on developing countries to continue their trade liberalization.

Perhaps the least development-friendly side of the Doha Declaration is its willingness to ladle out "special and defferential treatment" without a perception of where developing Members would be better off if *they themselves* observed the disciplines the negotiations [illegible]h to establish. On this score the Declaration comes close to getting it backward; soft on trade liberalization by developing countries where it should be hard, insistent on expanding trade negotiations into new areas of behind-the-border policies and institutions, where the Uruguay Round indicates that trade negotiations provide a troubled approach to development. On services liberalization the Declaration got it right: it follows the Uruguay Round mode.

At the Uruguay Round the trade community addressed itself to several aspects of economic structure that have important development dimensions. On services, the trade negotiators'casualness to the relevant economics has not been a problem because the agreement allows each party to work out the relevant economics step-by-step. In other areas, where the Uruguay Round imposed generic legal obligations, there are problems. The agreement on intellectual property rights is a glaring example. Knowledge is critical for development. Helping people earn more from knowledge and depend less on muscle is a noble objective. Building property rights in poor countries is critical for odevelopment.[19] There has to be however a better way to do it than to tell developing countries that they owe $60 billion/year for which they get nothing in return. That is the TRIPS legal reality. The Uruguay Round may have set back rather than advanced the formation of commercial constituencies in developing countries that would benefit from a higher standard of intellectual property rights.

Development institutions must lead here. On subjects such as standards and intellectual property the development institutions' approach is more appropriate than the trade negotiators'. Development institutions are more comfortable with the (dull) technicalities of project design and cost-benefit analysis. Their legalities—that follow rather than lead project design—are country-specific and project-specific, more suited to the one-off problems and trial-error rhythm of what is needed here than is WTO's generic approach to legal obligation.

Two guidelines to ensure that trade negotiations advance development:

(i) Apples for apples;

(ii) All reciprocity is local.

Grand bargains over wide spans do not work, particularly bargains in which what you pay is written into the contract, and what you get will come from "economics."Rubens Ricupero (2000) was on the right track, he noticed that the promised technical assistance in the Uruguay Round new areas was unbound. He did not however go far enough, he overlooked that the *economic benefits themselves* were unbound. First, make sure the benefits are as legally bound as the costs, then see that the frills such as adjustment assistance are also legally bound. Do not trust trade ministers when they talk about money, they do not have any. In tariff negotiations each country's costs are in the same coin as its benefits, one as legally bound as the other. GATS allows the same, stick with that model.

The softness in TRIPS and other agreements that take the form of generic obligations over behind-the-border regulations and institutions is more than creative ambiguity. It is reality. TRIPS regulations that relate to domestic institutions and rules are necessarily flexible because reform needs differ across countries. It is not technically or otherwise possible to address in a one-size-fits-all way the specific needs of many different countries. If this mode of agreement is proposed for additional areas of behind-the-border regulations and institutions, Members should be aware that "project design" becomes then the turning of legal obligations into commercial realities. That activity depends on the business skills of the commercial constituencies with interests at stake. Commercial, not just diplomatic interests must be brought to bear early–on negotiations that create the legal obligations that commercial skills later turn into commercial realities. The shift of power from diplomacy to business is not easy—it took the US Congress 25 years to reorient the US delegation. Those that have accomplished the shift will dominate future negotiations.

An agenda of agriculture, industrial tariffs, and services would have considerable potential. In each part each party would gain from its own concessions as well as from those of others. This is the situation in which traditional trade negotiations have done a lot of good in the past. Remember, the contribution of trade negotiations stems from their capacity to overcome the political incorrectness of good economics, not from their capacity to supply good economics.

A broad agenda, some argue, is needed to provide something for everyone, but this is contradicted by GATT's history. The domestic politics of winners versus losers will not support it. Furthermore, a broad exchange is not necessarily a positive one. A broad agenda can trade nothing for nothing as well as something for something. If the developed countries put in competition policy only to have a "receivable" to nullify their "payable" on agriculture, shame on them.

Financial negotiations recognize that the subject is money and they send the accountants first. The diplomats do not come until the parties agree on the numbers, and diplomats not comfortable talking to accountants do not come. Trade negotiators, Run the numbers! Particularly if you stray into behind-the-border matters, Run the numbers. Draw on commercial constituencies and on Ministries who have operational responsibilities in the areas being negotiated. In tariff negotiations each country's costs are in the same coin as its benefits, one as legally bound as the other. GATS allows the same, stick with that model.

Development institutions, Get into the game. If there is momentum behind the development dimensions of the new areas, then the trade dimensions can be managed; but one cannot push the string. Run the numbers. This is about money, not diplomacy.

REFERENCES

1. I confess here a semantic debt to Robert E. Hudec, particularly to his classic article " The GATT Legal System: A Diplomat's Jurisprudence" (Hudec 1970).

2. The cuts covered approximately 30 pre cent each of developed and developing country imports (by value, vis-à-vis Uruguay Round base

1986-1988). Developing country importers will save on average 2.3 per cent of the cost of imports; developed country importers, 1 per cent. Uruguay Round bindings cover 88 percent of developed country imports, by value; 81 per cent of developing country imports (again per Uguguay Round base 1986-1988 imports.) The cuts and bindings were tabulated from WTO Integrated Data Base Statistics; details are provided in Finger, Ingco, and Reincke (1996).

3. A survey of different analyses of the Uruguay Round outcome found estimates that ranged from $50 billion to $150 billion.

4. Estimates are of strictly the effects of reciprocal negotiations agreed at the Uruguay Round. They exclude any unilateral liberalization that might have been implemented by Members (e.g., Latin American countries) during the negotiations. People's Republic of China (PRC) was not a member during the Uruguay Round negotiations, so estimates do not include any liberalization PRC may have undertaken; PRC is included strictly as a concession receiver.

5. Preeg (1995) and Feketekuty (1988) document the industrial origins of the services and intellectual property negotiations; Shaffer (2002) focuses on the interaction of enterprises and negotiators.

6. The matter is elaborated in Finger (2001) and Winters (2002).

7. There are, of course, distributional issues (winners and losers) within countries. Real economics does not suggest that trade liberalization will not have domestic losers as well as domestic winners, only that the gains will generally exceed the losses.

8. IIPA is a private sector coalition comprised of six trade associations whose members are some 1,100 US companies who produce and distribute copyright-protected materials throughout the world.

9. See Maskus (2000) and World Bank (2002).

10. No doubt enterprises in other countries are as capable as US enterprises to identify sales opportunities that foreign adherence to WTO obligations might provide, and that other governments, like the US government, have ways to work with such enterprises. Indeed, the creation by the US Congress of the Industry Consultations Programme and such instruments as Section 301 was motivated by a perception that foreign trade negotiators did a better job of advancing the commercial interests of their enterprises than did US negotiators. We have not yet had the opportunity to study such mechanisms in other countries.

11. I acknowledge another semantic debt, this time to Tip O'Neil (1995) from his book titled *All Politics Is Local.*

12. Zeller (1992) provides examples of the trades US President John F. Kennedy made to win Congressional approval of the authority

to negotiate in what came to be called the Kennedy Round. Providing quota protection for the textile industry was part of it; an extensive waterways project for the state of Oklahoma was another part.

13. Building on user constituencies has never worked in trade politics, it would be particularly difficult with intellectual property because the TRIPS agreement imposes a burden on users, not a benefit.
14. Under provisions of the Uruguay Round Agreements, negotiations on agriculture and services began in early 2000. The Doha Agenda incorporates these and adds negotiations on other issues.
15. The escalating legal cost of maneuvering within them does have the existential effect of disciplining use by pricing out smaller industries.
16. Finger (1993) elaborates this point.
17. Finger, Ng, and Wangchuk (2001) document the point and explore its implications.
18. The last item is from the call in the WTO Singapore Ministerial Declaration of 1996 for a Plan of Action for the least developing countries and for the creation of the Integrated Framework among multilateral institutions
19. Hernando de Soto (1990) makes the case well.

APPENDIX

Summary Content: Doha Ministerial Declaration Work Programme

1. Negotiations

Agriculture

1. Negotiations aimed at substantial improvements of *market access,* reductions, with a view to phasing out, all forms of *export subsidies,* substantial reductions of trade-distorting *domestic support;*
2. without prejudging the outcome of the negotiations;
3. allow developing countries to take into account development needs including food security and rural development;
4. taking non-trade concerns into account is confirmed; and
5. special and differential treatment shall be an integral part...embodied in the schedules of concessions...in the rules and disciplines....so as to be operationally effective.

Market Access for Non-agricultural Products

1. Negotiations shall aim to reduce or eliminate tariffs, tariff peaks, high tariffs, tariff escalation, non-tariff barriers;

2. in particular on products of export interest to developing countries; and
3. less than full reciprocity from developing and least developed countries;
4. Modalities will include *studies and capacity-building measures to assist least developed countries* to participate effectively in negotiations.

Services

1. With a view to promote economic growth of all members, the development of developing and least developed countries;
2. previously agreed guidelines and procedures are reaffirmed; and
3. participants shall submit initial requests by 30 June 2002, initial offers by 31 March 2003.

Trade-Related Aspects of Intellectual Property Rights

1. Ministers stress the importance of implementation and interpretation supportive of public health...adopt a separate Declaration....;
2. agree to negotiate a multilateral system of notification and registration of geographic indicators for wines and spirits; and
3. extension of protection of geographic indicators will be addressed in the TRIPS Council.
4. Ministers instruct the TRIPS Council to examine the relation between TRIPS and the Convention on Biological Diversity, the protection of traditional knowledge and folklore....

Relationship between Trade and Investment, Interaction between Trade and Competition Policy, Transparency in Government Procurement, Trade Facilitation:

1. Negotiations will take place after the Fifth Ministerial, by explicit consensus, according to modalities adopted there;
2. Until the Fifth Ministerial the relevant Working Group or Council will continue preparatory work on scope and definition, modalities etc.;
3. Ministers support technical assistance and capacity building;
4. Negotiations on government procurement explicitly limited to transparency, not to restrict the scope for countries to give preferences to domestic supplies and suppliers.

WTO Rules

1. Clarify and improve disciplines under the anti-dumping and subsidies and countervailing measures agreements; and
2. preserve basic concepts and objectives of these agreements and their instruments;
3. Clarify and improve disciplines on fisheries subsidies; on WTO provisions on regional agreements.

4. Take into account development needs of developing countries (mentioned three times in the section)

Dispute settlement Understanding

1. Negotiations on improvements and clarifications.

Trade and Environment

1. Negotiations without prejudging their outcome;
2. on procedures for information exchange between Secretariats of multilateral environmental agreements (MEAs) and WTO;
3. on relationship between WTO rules and trade obligations in MEAs; (limited to the impact of existing WTO rules among parties to the MEA in question);
4. on reduction or elimination of tariff and non-tariff barriers on environmental goods and services; and
5. include identification of any need to clarify WTO rules.

Electronic Commerce

1. Ministers agree to continue the *Work Programme* on electronic commerce; and
2. declare that Members will maintain their current practice of not imposing customs duties on electronic transmissions until the Fifth Ministerial.

II. Continuing Consideration (Not Negotiations)

Small Economies

1. Ministers agree to a work programme under the General Council; and
2. to further integrate small, vulnerable economies into the multilateral trading system, not to create a WTO subcategory.

Trade, Debt, and Finance

1. Ministers agree to examination in a Working Group under the General Council, of the relationship among trade, debt, and finance; and
2. strengthen coherence of international trade and financial policies.

Trade and Transfer of Technology

1. Ministers agree to examination in a Working Group under the General Council of the relationship between trade and transfer of technology.

III. Cross-Cutting Considerations

Implementation-Related Issues and Concerns

1. Where there is a negotiating mandate implementation issues will be an integral part of the negotiations; and
2. other implementation issues to be addressed as a matter of priority in the relevant WTO bodies.

Technical Cooperation and Capacity Building

1. Confirm that technical cooperation and capacity building are core elements of the development dimension of the multilateral trading system;
2. Instruct the Secretariat with other agencies to support domestic efforts to mainstream trade into development, poverty reduction strategies;
3. WTO technical assistance is to assist developing and transition countries to adjust to WTO rules and disciplines, implement obligations, and exercise the rights of membership, including drawing on the benefits.

Least Developed Countries

1. Ministers recognize the needs for market access, support for technical assistance, capacity building, diversification of production, and export structures;
2. welcome past market access improvements and commit to consider additional market access;
3. agree to work to facilitate and accelerate negotiations with acceding least developed countries (LDCs);
4. endorse the Integrated Framework and urge development partners to increase contributions to the Integrated Framework trust fund; and
5. instruct the Subcommittee for LDCs to design and report at work programme consistent with the WTO mandate adopted at the Third UN Conference on LDCs.

Special and Differential Treatment

1. Ministers reaffirm that special and differential treatment is an integral part of WTO agreements; and
2. agree that special and differential treatment provisions shall be reviewed with a view to strengthening them and making them more precise, effective and operational.

Note: This interpretation is intended to be explanatory but has no official standing. All questions about meaning of the Declaration should refer to the text of the Declaration.

5

Is Copyright on the Wrong Track?

What is the purpose of intellectual property rights? Originally they were based on the principle that creators should be granted exclusive rights to exploit their works, in order to ensure they were properly remunerated and, in addition, to encourage creative activity. But in the interest of the community and of future artists and inventors, those exclusive rights were limited in time: when the term of protection ran out, the works fell into the public domain, a copyright-free space that encourages creation and competition. They could then be used as raw material and a kind of "suggestion box" by fresh generations of creators. A balance between the protection of individual property and the general interest was guaranteed.

Today that balance has been destroyed. The founding principles of intellectual property seem to be threatened by an ill considered increase in the number of privately held exclusive rights at the expense of the public domain.

Counterfeit Software and Designer Clothes

The main factor hastening these developments is a change in the economy, which focuses increasingly on products with "intellectual added value", such as new software the selection and presentation of information, specialized computer services, cultural and entertainment products, biotech products, and other applications of cutting-edge technologies. Control of ideas, forms, images and brands is a crucial element in this so-called "immaterial economy".

While it is difficult to steal a consignment of steel girders or a cargo of bananas, it is child's play to copy software or manufacture counterfeit designer clothes. It is easy for intellectual added value to be illicitly appropriated: it cannot be "put under lock and key". Those who want to exploit it for their own profit simply need to be able to reproduce it. Pirates in this field can market copied products at a lower price than the originals, since they do not have to pay the cost of creating or advertising the product. By doing this, they distort competition.

International Negotiations

To protect their industries against piracy and counterfeiting, the member countries of GATT (General Agreement of Tariffs and Trade, which governed international trade from 1947 to 1994) set out to strengthen intellectual property rights within the GATT framework. GATT's main concern was to protect companies from unauthorized copying and unfair competition, thus ensuring they would get a return on their investment.

What GATT concluded it first agreements, intellectual property was not very high on the agenda. In the immediate postwar years, products put on the market still consisted of atoms of matter, not bytes. It was not until the Uruguay Round of talks started in 1986 that the issue came to be discussed at the international level. That round of talks resulted in the signing, on April 15 1994, of the agreement on Trade-Related Aspects of Intellectual Property Rights (TRIPS). Like the multilateral agreements on trade in goods, the text was included in an appendix to the Marrakesh framework agreement that set up GATT's successors, the World Trade Organization (WTO).

TRIPS, which has a global application (most countries in the world have now subscribed to it), confirmed the economic importance of intellectual property rights. It requires member states to protect all forms of creation: literary and artistic work in the broadest sense (including maps and press photos). Computer programmes, data bases, sound recordings, radio and television broadcasts, drawings and models, inventions of products and processes in every technological field, the lay-out designs of integrated circuits, and so on.

The agreement was a milestone in the history of intellectual property. First, its scope of application is unprecedentedly wide: anything created in the fields of technology, scftware, news or culture can and must be protected by an intellectual property right, in such a way that it exclusively benefits rights holders, who alone decide how it should be reproduced and distributed. Secondly, for the first time TRIPS requires contracting states to organize procedures and sanctions that enable rights holders to ensure that their rights are respected. Those states are for example obliged to allow persons or companies. Whose rights have been infringed upon to go court and obtain damages. Such duties are chiefly incumbent upon the developing countries. Most of these countries do not possess the human or financial resources that would enable them to develop their own production, and they have tended to become the preferred locations of the copying industries.

A New Right to Protect Investment

Financial interests again have prompted to consider the adoption of a directive on the protection of biotechnological inventions. The move was motivated by two factors: first, "the protection of biotechnological inventions will certainly be of key importance for the Community's industrial development", secondly, "research and development, notably in the field of genetic engineering, require a considerable degree of high-risk investment which cannot be profitable unless there is adequate legal protection".

Financial terminology—talk of profitability and an attractive "return on investment"—is invading the sphere of intellectual property. The notion of intellectual property used to be a way of protecting intellectual added value, it has now become an instrument for turning invested capital to good account. Is this a necessity or is it regrettable? The question is worth debating.

It is true that in the field of biotechnology, for example, creation requires considerable investment. This is something that industrial companies cannot accept unless they are sure of being able to make it at least partially profitable. On the other hand, one may reasonably wonder whether there is any point in creating a new monopoly on information contained in data bases, even if a great deal of time and money has gone into creating them. The idea here is not to reward an intellectual creation, however slight, but merely to repay an investment in time and money. This trend could well jeopardize the sharing of knowledge. The notion on intellectual property here seems to have departed from its basic purpose, which was to ensure a balance between private and public interests.

This change of direction is one of the first perverse effects of the exponential increase in the amount of space occupied by intellectual property. More fundamentally, it has been engineered by a society that tends to make legal and material protection the keystone of its ethos; all property and anything else of value needs to be protected against risk. Accident prevention, security, insurance and protection have become mantras in developed Western societies. It has reached the point where those societies sometimes seem to have forgotten that risk is an inherent aspect of life and freedom. The second perverse effect of the boom in intellectual property—the broadening of its scope as well as of its duration—is equally worrying.

On many occasions over the last ten years, legislators and courts have also agreed to an unlimited extension of the scope of copyright protection. Originally designed to protect works of art, copyright has been extended to cover every sphere to human creation, from the design of car bodywork or ties, meteorological photographs and the instruction manuals of electrical household appliances to data bases and receipts. Since everything belongs to someone, an authorization from the owner is required for everything. In practice it has become extremely difficult to crate a multimedia work, to shoot a film, to compose a piece of music, or to publish an illustrated book without in someway having to use elements that are protected by copyright, and therefore having to request a detailed authorization from copyright holders and to pay them financial compensation.

In the short term, this increase in the number of exclusive rights will be a threat to economic activity itself. Competition, after all, boils down to offering the same product as someone else. Now if that product and all its variants, versions and components are protected by intellectual copyright, copying—in other words, making a competing offer—becomes an extremely hazardous exercise. If limited exclusive rights, which used to form part of the original spirit of intellectual property, protect companies against illicit copying, disproportionate exclusive rights quite simply wipe out competition altogether.

As for the extension of the duration of copyright, if means that the community's right to make free use of a work after it has fallen into the public domain will be a theoretical possibility rather than a fact. The present duration of copyright protection often exceeds the period during which the created work is in fact usable. After 70 years or more, an old computer programme is of no use to any one.

Similarly, the European directive on data bases theoretically restricts their protection period to 15 years. But it stipulates that if a data base is modified, notably by a large number of additions, deletions or changes which show there has been substantial further investment, the duration can be extended by 15 years. Thus, a regularly updated data base can be protected for ever and will therefore never fall out of copyright. That contravenes the most fundamental principles that underlay the notion of intellectual property rights.

6

Add Value, Go Global

Can Southern Firms Break into Export Markets?

The global economy has changed beyond recognition over the last decade. Widespread economic policy reform and in particular trade liberalization have opened up new opportunities for developing countries. In poor countries, however, the consequences of trade liberalization are not always positive. What can the private sector do to respond better and make the most of new trading opportunities? What factors have limited the impact of economic reforms on export performance?

Why have exports from poorer countries failed to increase more rapidly following trade liberalization? What can be done to improve performance? Research on the response of firms in the private sector to economic reform can underpin new approaches to export promotion for poorer developing countries. For a long time, protective trade policies, poorly performing state-owned industries and state controls over the private sector were blamed for poor export performance in Africa and South Asia. Now that some of these problems have been remedied, other obstacles have come to light.

The effect of economic liberalization and adjustment on the performance of poor countries has been cause for concern. Trade liberalization should increase incentives to export and facilitate business enterprise by encouraging private ownership through privatization and by attracting foreign investment. Macro-economic stability ought to boost business confidence and performance. All these factors should promote exports, offsetting job and income losses caused by the closure or reorganization of inefficient enterprises and industries yet, although some degree of reform and stability it is without export growth that was expected.

Trade reform and macro-economic stability may be necessary conditions for improved export performance but by them are insufficient. The obstacles to improving export performance are numerous and there is no easy policy answer. The research programme examined export performance at three levels:

- *Regional:* How trade strategies should vary with skills and natural resource endowments;
- *National:* Factors influencing the export performance of manufacturing;
- *Sectoral:* The performance of particular sectors of the economy.

The East Asian economies have shown that developing countries can complete successfully in global markets. For many, they provide a blueprint for economic growth applicable to many, poor countries.

South Asia's comparative advantage lies in its abundant unskilled labour, while Africa's lies in its abundant natural resources. Different export promotion strategies are essential. South Asia's best prospectus are in labour-intensive manufacturing: the region's low level of exports would soar over the next decade if current obstacles to trade were reduced. Africa's exports could also increase but its biggest potential in primary products that need little educated labour and abundant natural resources.

Some African countries could also be substantial exporters of manufacturers, but their actual manufactured exports in most cases now fall far short. Comparing Ghana to Mauritius—one of Africa's most successful exporters of manufactured goods differences in firm-level efficiency are apparent Mauritian firms have more capital per worker and use it more efficiently. Reducing trade barriers is not sufficient. Wages in Ghana would have to be substantially lower to offset low labour productivity. Alternatively, labour productivity will have to be drastically improved if Ghanian firms are to compete successfully in export markets with wages at current levels.

Even when companies use capital and labour efficiently, poor infrastructure is a frequent stumbling products to export markets—an acute problem in landlocked countries and equally acute for manufacturers as research on Uganda clearly shows. What huts manufacturing exporters is being hit by the high cost of transporting their output to foreign markets and of transporting the materials they need from abroad. The cost penalties resulting from geography and poor infrastructure are far greater in Uganda than from high tariffs and other import restrictions.

Southern firms can still break into export markets, however, Developing-country firms do export to markets with exacting standards for product quality, reliability of delivery, and consumer safety. Two crucial aspects, however, are often overlooked:

- Non-manufacturing sectors, such as tourism and horticulture, generate significant employment and offer opportunities for supplying increasingly sophisticated products. Although manufacturing is considered more attractive, certain areas of tourism and horticulture can be equally appealing;
- New export opportunities are created as southern producers establish closer links with foreign customers. Producers of labour-intensive products such as garments, horticulture and footwear frequently depend on large retailers and specialist international traders for designs, information about demand and technical support.

Supermarkets make key decisions about which fruit and vegetables to grow, how they should be produced and processed and which firms should be included in the business.

Strategic decisions by international producers and retailers in the footwear industry have been crucial in developing new production locations such as Vietnam and Romania. Similarly, work on automotive components production in South Africa and India illustrates how global sourcing by the leading motor companies closes off some markets and opens up others. Export prospects can only be evaluated in the light of global restructuring in these industries.

Emphasising global linkages does not mean that developing countries are powerless in the face of global forces. Even in tightly-structured industries, there is scope for national policy and national strategy. Further more, there are important export sectors that are not structured in this way. Some tourism is dominated by large northern firms and is heavily import-dependent, but there is also enormous potential and national policy will be crucial in shaping the industry and its contribution to the economy as a whole.

For southern firms to break into export markets, certain issues must be addressed, especially in Africa. Some are recognized as important policy issues—investing in human capital and improving infrastructure for example. As one set of constraints are reduced—such as removing policy—induced distortions through trade liberalization—another set takes precedence. In response to the integration of global markets, southern producers must join the global distribution chains to ensure markets for their exports.

These findings impose hard choices on developing countries. Should a firm allocated limited funds for investment in human capital or investment infrastructure? Future research might contribute by quantifying relative rates of return. On another level, countries may worry about the independence and autonomy of local producers if they are to join a global chain typically donated by northern companies. Rules regulate governmental trade and investment policies but who controls the global buyers and multinational companies whose decisions have such huge impacts on developing countries?

7

Richer or Poorer?

Achievements and Challenges of Ethical Trade

Ethical trade as an approach to supply chain management has mushroomed in recent years. Northern companies are becoming increasingly concerned with the 'ethics' of their operations and the risks to reputation and productivity posed by bad employment practices in global supply chains. But can voluntary private sector codes really improve employment conditions in supply chains?

Ethical trade is one dimension of corporate social responsibility, bringing social issues into the mainstream of commercial supply chain management through the use of codes of conduct. It is sometimes confused with fair-trade which addresses terms of trading for smaller producers, and fosters greater responsibility in supply chain relations.

Ethical trade, on the other hand, focuses on workplace issues, requiring that supplier's in particular meet minimum employment, worker welfare and aspects of human rights standards.

Similar management systems are well established for product safety and environmental issues, Here, we focus on the social dimensions of ethical trade and its codes of conduct yet the separation of social and environment standards is increasingly artificial in global sourcing agreements. A plethora of codes are on offer. The most numerous are in-houses codes such as Nike's 233 company codes were counted in 1999 and the figure is rising.

Suppliers have to comply with and pay for a multitude of similar but different codes. Harmonising codes or establishing equivalence is on the agenda but has not yet halted the problem of 'code overload'.

At a broader level, industry-specific codes have also been developed. The US Apparel industry Partnership/Fair Labour Agreement adopted by a number of leading US merchandising companies is a good example. Industry standards are not new, as ISO and EMAS environmental management systems show, Building on ISO principles, Social Accountability International (formerly CEPAA) has developed SA8000. This is an independent social standard that can be used as an auditable code throughout the private sector.

Ethical trade is partly a response to consumer and campaigning group pressure in globalised economy. Alliances of companies, NGOs, trade. Developing codes of conduct through a multi stakeholder approach is a striking aspect of ethical trade, bringing together companies, NGOs, trade unions and some government departments. An example of this collaborative approach is the Ethical Trading Initiative (ETI) in the UK. The ETI's baseline code of conduct that corporate members from various industries must comply with as a minimum standard is more than just a code, ETI aims to provide a learning environment and sponsors pilot projects in developing countries to test different methods of monitoring and verification.

Codes of conducts need to be assessed in terms of content, implantation and impact. A number of professional auditing companies have moved into this area, some accredited to audit specific codes such as FLA or SA8000. Suppliers audited against a specific code undergo an inspection, and where non-compliance is found, have to take remedial action or risk failing the audit.

Social auditing is complex process, however, and it can be difficult to spot work place abuse, such as sexual harassment or forced overtime, Workers have little confidence in a process that appears to be linked with management, and fear that reporting issues could risk their jobs. Advocates of the multi-stakeholder approach argue that effective monitoring and verification of codes must involve local NGOs and trade unions in which workers have trust. Participatory social auditing, also a means of raising awareness and of facilitating behavioural change, can help reveal serious management problems. But in many developing countries local organizations lack the capacity of participate: developing sustainable local systems of monitoring and verification remains an important challenge.

Do the advantages of multi-stakeholder approaches outweigh immediate constraints? Ethical trade is a largely northern driven process, reflecting Western ethical thinking and priorities, Southern based initiatives, however, are expanding, raising the possibility of local ownership of codes, Collaboration poses challenges. Stronger relationships and better understanding are essential between southern and northern workers, producers, trade unions, and NGOs for codes to work globally.

But there is still skepticism as to the extent of the benefits that ethical trade might bring. Will increasing southern capacity to participate, as the ETI has done in its pilot project, help? Will building trust, confidence and dialogue achieve the objectives of ethical trade, north and south? Child labour is often more complex, however, than codes make it appear. Codes need to address the conditions of all workers within the supply chain, including the least visible: partnerships must include all groups to address these limitations.

The role of government is hotly contested. Can a system whose credibility depends on under-resourced civil society actors, often excluding democratically elected representatives, maintain genuine credibility? If the boundaries between private sector and public sector roles are not defined, the list of private sector responsibilities will become unmanageable. Private sector initiatives are not a substitute for more comprehensive national or international development policies.

What are the consequences of codes? Do they encourage downsizing or reinforce from large suppliers where compliance is more easily monitored? There is a risk that the gains of some will be at the expense of others.

Ethical trade has successfully begun forging partnerships to find solutions. While it might be wrong to assume that ethical trade can change the world, handled wisely it could make a world of difference for some. Yet it is not a panacea for development. Issues that remain unchallenged by ethical trade include:

- The exclusion of companies producing for domestic markets—often bigger employers.
- Underlying causes of poverty and social marginalisation.

8

Challenging Traditional Economic Growth

Today, saving the planet is about redefining our economic development models. Striving towards the fulfillment of basic human rights is an integral part of environmental protection. Without a people-centered development strategy we will fail. Conflicting interests and lack of vision and courage are among the many reasons why its is so hard to meet needs in a world of plenty. We are faced with three major challenges in the 1990s:

- to curb population growth and poverty;
- to search for sustainable production and consumption patterns;
- to promote equity.

Population growth is often associated with poverty. But who causes the major strain on the environment? The 1.2 billion poorest people consume small amounts of the world's resources and contribute little to harmful emissions. They do not cause a heavy burden. The day-to-day struggle for survival of the poorest does, however, undermine their resources, and this causes deaths as population grows beyond the carrying capacity of nature. Here two key elements are essential: to turn from non-renewable to renewable resources, and to minimize use of resources through resource efficiency. We must single out the products and processes that must be phased out and those which may be allowed to expand. Right prices that include the ecological costs will be explored further, together with administrative measures. We are ready to examine the possibilities of using "green tax" reforms to enhance employment and harness pollution and inefficient resources use. By shifting the burden of taxes from labour to environmentally harmful products and processes we might achieve a double benefit.

Transport, waste management, energy and land use are obvious areas that need to be affected by policy changes. Individuals must use their power as green-conscious citizens and shoppers—but, in the end, producers and service providers hold the main key to practical action.

The market must be harnessed to meet people's needs both for present and future generations—starting by making economic policies play by the rules of nature. The World Trade Organization (WTO) negotiations have provided us with instruments to regulate world trade.

Getting the Prices Right

Car emissions may be cut drastically, but the rapid increase of new cars nullifies the benefits. Even the most ardent technological optimist must admit that we need new priorities or cuts in some products and services. For example, we must improve public transport and resource-efficient cars—and reduce traffic.

Traditional economic growth models fall short of solving the problem of unemployment. Indeed, 'robots' and wasteful resource use replace people. There are great job-creating possibilities in environment-friendly produces and processes. Striving towards equity within and between nations, and within and between generations, is the major challenge of our time.

The fact that 20 per cent of the world's population consumes 80 per cent of the world's resources has too long been seen as mainly an ethical challenge. Ethics are not essily translated into politics, especially when confronted with economic and market realities. As equity gradually becomes a security issue—as it will, if we do not bridge the gaps within and between nations—it will climb to the top of the political agenda.

Many of the main conflict areas of today are battlefields of resource management. These will expand greatly if we do not turn conference statements of good intension into action. The 30-year old commitment of the rich countries to meet the target of 0.7 per cent of GNP in official Development Assistance remains unmet.

Two hundred years of Western-led development optimism reached its peak in the late 1980s. When the Berlin wall fell, the economic growth models of the rich countries had become the universal recipe. But as more and more people aspire to join the ranks of the middle classes, the resulting environmental stress calls for a halt, or a radical change of course.

The call for new patterns of production and consumption challenges our traditional concepts of economic growth and the focus on materialism in our culture. Neither the industrialized nor the poorer countries are strangers to radical process of change, through the reasons for change are shifting. And we are truly facing challenging and conflict-provoking changes.

No nation by itself can solve the problems we face. Pollution knows no frontiers, but comes to us with the winds and waves. We have become more and more interdependent. If we are to attain sustainable development, we must commit ourselves through international agreements, through an international rule of law, through the development of financial mechanisms and through institutional agreements. We must develop means and tools to enhance collective security and mutual interests.

9

Unemployment in the Poor and Rich Worlds

Different Causes, but Converging Policies?

In view of the magnitude of global unemployment, all the customary formulas offered by economists against mass unemployment—the basic socio-economic problem of modern times—appear to the quackery. Neither quantitative, nor any kin of 'qualitative', growth will be able to eliminate the disastrous worldwide lack of jobs. For ecological reasons it is impossible to include 800 million or more unemployed in the production process through corresponding growth. The resulting increase in global Gross Domestic Product would require consumption of natural resources, energy and the environment which, given even the greatest possible productivity in those sectors, could not even be sustained for two or three decades.

In addition, aiming to achieve full employment through growth will be ever more difficult even in the rich economies. For it is most likely that work productivity will continue to rise worldwide. Countries such as China, which are in the initial phase of modernization, are still producing at a relatively still low productivity rate. But that is precisely why they can achieve notable increases in productivity in a short time by importing technology from highly-developed countries. The advantage of rapid 'catch-up rationalisation', however, is being bought at the cost of rising unemployment and progressive impoverishment.

Employment Through Redistribution of Work

The notion that jobs can at some time be created for 800-900 million unemployed who will work 35 or even 40 hours a week at the productivity level of the highly-developed countries of four or five decades ago is absurd. The only realistic possibility of eliminating the world's unemployment problem is by far-reaching redistribution of work and income. The change needed for that demands fundamentally new concepts of prosperity: a reflection on the philosophy of the 'life of happiness'. 'New concepts of prosperity' means that technological progress would no longer be used mainly to deliver rising per capita income and excessive consumption. Instead, given a sufficient material standard of living, the quality of life would be improved primarily by shortening working hours. It is about, so to speak, assigning instrumental good sense new goals. Plus reshaping socio-economic conditions in such a way that the politicians will again be compelled to orient themselves on the good of the community and humanistic values instead of filling the pockets of the wealthy. It is sheer ideology, although very persuasive, to cite 'globalization' and its alleged 'iron laws' in defaming the welfare state, full employment and social justice as out-of-date wishful thinking. A return to the state-guided social competitive system as practised during the first decades after the Second World War is possible just as it was politically feasible to make the transition from the old order of unfettered. Ruthless capitalism to the mixed economies of the social market economy types. So it is a matter of restoring the proven structures of a mixed economic system.

However, in contrast to the first post-war decades it is now not sufficient to regenerate nation-state interventionism. Appropriate international regulations are required. Above all, it will depend upon reversing the new laissez-faire developments in international economic relationships which today are subsumed under the buzzward 'globalisation'. That is, to oppose over-liberalisation and its disastrous social and inhuman impacts. It will depend on the broad mobilisation of the losers in the process of globalisation whether the necessary fundamental change of course can still be made in time before a catastrophe. In particular, the new myth must be opposed that declares globalisation as a kind of law of nature and thus suggests resignation and adaptation to an allegedly unavoidable process of destruction of social and human achievements.

Mass Unemployment in the Poor Economies

The employment problems in the rich and the poor hemispheres differ not only in their magnitude, but also in their causes. The wretched condition of the poor economies is due above all to historical reasons: colonialism and, in the post-colonial era, the constraints to independent development imposed by the hegemonic influence of the rich industrial states. The waste of scarce resources by international and civil wars, and the dictatorships with their upperclass luxury consumption and inefficient, thus development–obstructing exploitation structures—often supported by the industrialized nations—have for a long time repressed and in many cases destroyed autonomous development potential. The colonial and post-colonial distortion also contributed at least indirectly to the current population problems of the poor countries. The politically inflicted mass poverty and under-development stabilized or in fact brought about economic, socio-psychological and ideological mechanisms which oppose an effective population policy. As we know, the average educational level in many developing countries, especially among women, is too low to give a modern population policy a chance of success. Mass unemployment in the poor countries is the result of poverty. In this respect, it is about a production-side problem: too few resources, too little real and human capital, and the inefficient, unproductive use of much of the anyway limited added value of society. The picture is totally different in the rich countries—the cover-production economies.

Unemployment in Over-Production Systems

The main cause of mass unemployment in the industrialized nations has nothing to do with shortages. It is a phenomenon of surplus. Greater possibilities of production can no longer be used 'sufficiently' profitably because the required demand is lacking. Production is done for profit. The necessary collateral condition is the satisfying of consumer needs. Employment is not even such a condition, but only a side effect which lapses immediately when labour-free production is technically possible. Thus, national income must be shared among wages and profits(or income form property). Profit is the difference between earnings and costs. Earnings depend upon demand. Macro-economic cost consist mainly of wages and salaries (including social security contributions). These definitive connections mean that profit can be made only if overall demand is greater than the total cost of labour. But in the final analysis this demand can only come from the profit-earners themselves. In his book, a Treatise on Money, Keynes described this nexus as the theory of the Widow's cruse. Under capitalistic conditions, labour is only sought or hired if profit can be earned with it. But as making a profit depends upon the demand for consumption and investment by the shareholders, it can be seen that the degree of employment is determined by the demand behaviour of the class that receives income from property. In this respect, the widespread belief that greater investment also leads to more employment, namely via the effect of investment in demand, is right.

Lower Wages Mean Lower Demand

The lower the level of wages, and given an unchanged total demand, the greater are the profits that can be made. But it is more likely that in the case of falling wages the overall demand will also drop. For stabilizing total demand would require the recipients of income from property to increase their spending on consumption and/or investment to the degree to which wages and the consumption based on them fell.

During the past 10 to 15 years the development of profits in most industrialized nations has been very favourable. But profits would have grown more strongly if the demand of the shareholders had been much greater. This would have created more employment at the same time. Thus, it can be assumed that the profits are simply too high for the shareholders to be able to go in for meaningful consumption or make profitable investments. That is the reason for the extreme redirection of capital from fixed assets to portfolio investment. The growth of speculative (unproductive) financial transactions during the 1980s and 1990s (buzzword: casino capitalism), corresponded with a relatively weak formation of real capital.

Wage rises, of course, narrow the scope for profit. But precisely this effect stimulated efforts to improve the profit situation not only by investment in rationalization, but also by investment in expansion aimed at the growing mass purchasing power. Since more is being invested, the profit mass also is growing according to the principle of the Widow's cruse. Too low wages, as it were, relieve the shareholders of the pressure to innovate and invest and allow them to earn their profits too easily. That is the real message of the 'purchasing power theory' of wages.

Over-Accumulation and Under-Consumption

Overproduction has two different causes which, however, mostly occur in tandem. They are over-investment, or creation of over-capacities, on the one hand, and lack of demand due to relative saturation and an absence of mass purchasing power on the other. But the main reason for mass unemployment in the rich hemisphere currently lies on the demand side. During the first three decades after the Second World War supply and demand rose in relative balance. Economic fluctuations showed up as temporary declines in generally positive GDP growth rates. These decades of (dynamic) balance of growth are often described today as the era of 'Fordism'. Its essential feature is that rising wages ensure continuing growth of consumption, so that equally growing profits also flow relatively continuously into investments to expand capacity and create jobs. The label 'Fordism' expresses the 'simple' view of the theory of the buying power of wages which is said to have been propagated by Henry Ford I. This was that his workers should earn enough to be above to buy the cars they made.

The astonishingly balanced development of supply and demand from 1950 to the mid-1970s was due above all to postwar reconstruction and the pent-up demand of consumers who were starved by wartime economy shortages. This stimulated positive investment sentiment, and high investments brought at the same time high profits. The postwar growth that led within a short time to full employment was also linked with growth in productivity which on multi-year average was more than twice that of the crisis period of the last 25 years. Thus, the so-called employment threshold (the GDP growth rate point at which employment growth begins) was much higher in those days than it is now, although there was full employment over a longer period. This simple fact opposes the thesis often propounded today that mass unemployment is above all related to rationalization. It is not rationalization per se, that is, progress that boosts productivity, which is the evil. The problem is that the mistakes in distribution policy which are rooted in capitalistic structures result in increases in supply encountering insufficient demand for goods, whereby the demand for labour drops. However, the fact that demand policy contradicts the requirements of a social ethic that is ecologically responsible and right for the interests of the poor countries was already spelled out. So if a demand–oriented growth policy is practised at all, it should be designed to be as environmentally compatible as possible. After all, there are possibilities for that, such as by expanding the production of services that spare resources. A one-hour driving lesson costs more energy than one hour of ballet instruction.

The politically initiated and implemented over-liberalisation and surrender of social prosperity to global competition since the 1970s, which reproduces the old self-destructive mechanism of laissez faire, have during the last two decades markedly accelerated the crisis development inherent in the system.

Summing Up, It is Noted That

- full employment in the rich economies would certainly be possible by means of demand policy, but only at a high cost to the environment that is concomitant with high growth rates;

- the growth policy of the rich countries impairs the poor economies' possibilities of medium to long-term growth, since these are falling back ever further in the competition for ever scarcer and thus ever more expensive resources;
- the environmental collapse currently expected for the third or fourth generation after us, which obviously also will trigger a collapse of the world economy and—probably ahead of that—armed conflicts which today are hardly imaginable, would happen very much sooner if economic growth were to be increased to such a degree that it would bring full employment worldwide;
- in the long term, the problem of global unemployment and global poverty can only be solved by a policy of massive redistribution, and in fact a redistribution, of work and income, whereby increases in productivity must be used mainly or only for shortening working hours. That is a demand which appears to be utopian. But utopias of today often have the quality of scripting the reality of tomorrow.

10

Taking a Lead in the Fight Against Poverty?

World Bank and IMF Speed Implementation of Their New Strategy

A change in development policy strategy in the poorest countries is at present being prepared with incredible speed. The IMF-style structural adjustment programmes that have been criticised for many years are being scrapped. The countries are now to take their own decisions on their paths to development. Their governments will no longer formulate poverty reduction programmes top-down, but in an intensive and long-term dialogue with societal groups and organizations. Governments and institutions of the North commit themselves to supporting these processes, such as by debt relief on an unprecedented scale. Dream or reality?

New Strategy Paper

Behind this euphoria lines a new abbreviation, PRSP, standing for Poverty Reduction Strategy Paper, which the IMF and World Bank invented last year. The G-7 countries in Cologne not only announced debt relief for the Heavily Indebted Poor Countries (HIPCs) but also demanded that it must serve above all for poverty reduction. The PRSP concept was then presented at the annual conference of the two Bretton Woods organizations.

The most important principles of the new "super weapon" in the fight against poverty are:

- PRSPs are papers, which describe the medium-term development paths of the poorest countries of the

South, particularly their strategies to combat poverty, and by this means enlist international support. A PRSP is not only the prerequisite for granting debt forgiveness in the context of the HIPC initiative. It is also necessary for all new IMF and World Bank loans to the so-called IDA countries, the some 70 poorest countries that receive concessional loans from the World Bank's International Development Agency (IDA). According to the World Bank, PRSPs should also be required for all future pledges of bilateral development assistance.

- Not only social sector programmes, but also the economic and financial policies of the developing countries are in future to be aimed at fighting poverty. Previously, the IMF always pronounced that a growth-oriented national economy and a far-reaching integration in the world market would have a trickle-down effect and also benefit the poor. Now the poor are to be asked what policies can help materially to improve their situation.
- PRSPs are to be developed on the basis of self-responsible country ownership. Accordingly, development and structural adjustment strategies are no longer to be developed by the Washington finance institutions, but the countries themselves.
- The heading "country ownership" is to underline that not only governments are called upon, PRSPs should come into being in a participatory process. That means involvement of trade unions, NGOs, cooperatives, associations, grass roots groups, political parties and parliaments. A country's PRSP should be developed in a societal debate, a dialogue between governments on one side and parliamentary, private sector and civil society on the other.

Rhetoric or Reality?

Are PRSPs the expression of a change of paradigm? In brief, if all what the papers contain is implemented in a consistent and wide-ranging way, the chances of achieving it are good but there are a number of open questions. The answers to them will have a bearing on success or failure.

- Is the IMF really changing its policy on the poorest countries or merely wrapping its old policy in new words? The growing criticism of the IMF in recent years strengthened latterly by the evaluation of the ESAF (Enhanced Structural Adjustment Facility) programmes, which once again proved their blatant weaknesses called for reaction and is now triggering changes—real or only rhetorical? There will be no more old-style ESAF loans based on macro-economic structural adjustment programmes. But the credit line remains, and is now called the Poverty Reduction and Growth Facility (PRGF). This will be granted on the basis of the PRSPs, which in each case must also be accepted by the IMF board of directors. How much influence will the IMF have on the design of the PRSPs? What happens if a government choose macro-economic strategies combat poverty which go against previous IMF policy? Open questions. Moreover, there is still no answer to the question of why the IMF is at all coming on with long-term and low-interest lines of credit in the poorest countries.

Mixed Feelings with Regard to World Bank Role

- Will the World Bank use the PRSP process to expand its own institutional power further? NGOs in the North and South are viewing this with mixed feelings. Many welcome the fact that for the moment the World bank appears to be asserting itself against its twin, the IMF. On the other hand 50 years of experience with World Bank strategies have certainly not strengthened their trust in the Bank's ability to make a convincing fight against poverty. That is why the EURODAD network also questions the role of the World Bank (and the IMF) in the PRSP process. It says the papers should not be presented to the two financial institutions, whose power over the development strategies of countries of the South thus would increase further. Rather, PRSPs should for example, be laid before a Round Table of all donors chaired by the United Nations Development Programme (UNDP).

Ownership

- The principles of developing countries being responsible for their own development strategies are as old as it is—in theory—right. There have been frequent complaints about shortcomings in ownership. But now, after decades of development strategies being set and structural adjustment programmes being dictated from outside, the governments of the poorest countries, which in many cases have only weak institutional capacities, can hardly taken on sole responsibility overnight. In addition, of course, not a few of the countries are ruled by corrupt political elites (promoted from outside over decades) that give little reason to hope they would immediately switch to poverty reduction politics. Scepticism and critical observation is justified even if there is no alternative to governments of the south taking over greater responsibility.
- Civil society actors are now asked to help out in particular in those countries whose governments appear to be less trustworthy. A nice idea that has little to do with real life. Civil society actors in developing countries in general and in the poorest countries in particular are extra-ordinarily weak institutions which in many cases are totally dependent on financing from the North.

The civil society landscape in other countries is even weaker. However, social actors in many countries would make useful contributions to developing sustainable strategies. But that calls for meaningful and lasting support, including financial support, capacity-building, and in some countries also political pressure to gain scope for societal engagement.

It is reasonable that not only the World Bank and other official donors but also, and above all, the northern NGO partners of these actors are now giving much thought to how civil societies in the south can be strengthened.

Participation?

Even assuming there were civil society actors capable of dialogue, that does not clarify what participation in the PRSP process is really supposed to mean. Is civil society only to be listened to, or can it if necessary refuse to approve a PRSP? What impact would a refusal have on acceptance of the document by the IMF and World Bank and other donor? And in view of the great time pressure, will civil society be at all able to formulate discuss and feed their positions into the process? It could be of dicisive importance for the current debate on the PRSP model to delink the urgently needed debt relief from drawing up a PRSP programme, which simply needs more time. For example, it is conceivable that there would be no great problems in granting a country a moratorium on debt servicing so long as a PRSP process is continuing and then for giving debt when it is completed. That would ease the time problem for NGOs and at the same time maintain pressure on governments actually to arrive at poverty reduction strategies that were developed in a particiυatory process.

Other Causes of Poverty in Developing Countries

The entire current process is focused on the countries of the south, their governments and societies. That diverts attention from the responsibility of the donors and creditors. Not only that the IMF's structural adjustment programmes to date have been counter-productive for fighting poverty (why does the IMF not admit that openly just for once?). Not only that the now promised debt reliefs are coming much too late (the debt crisis of the poorest countries was deplored decades ago!). The present strategy also ignores various other exogenous causes of poverty in the South. What impacts do the finance and trade policies of northern countries have on the modest attempts to enable sustainable development in the South? What consequences will the continuing cutting of development budgets have on the South (no one anyway ventures to talk nowadays about the old 0.7 per cent ODA-GNP ratio)? Fort the donors and creditors to now pass the buck of sole responsibility to the governments of the South and present themselves in the background as noble do-gooders may be a successful strategy in terms of domestic politics, but not an acceptable one for development policy.

11

Consumption Bomb

It is three decades since we passed the peak world population growth rate of 2.04 per cent. Annual additions too are now a decade past their peak of 86 Million a year. They are currently running at 78 Million a year and are heading downwards. A peak in total numbers, however, still lies at least four or five decades ahead. On the UN Population Division's 1998 projections, the total is likely to reach 8.9 billion in 2050. The long range medium projection, which has not been updated since 1996, axpects world population to level out at just under 11 billion in 2200 AD.

However, this is based on assumptions that are increasingly questionable. More and more countries are reaching levels of female fertility that are not enough for replacement—below 2.1 children over the life time of each women. At the latest count there are 61 countries in this category. Of this 23 had very low fertility, below 1.5.

This situation is unprecedented in times of global peace on economic growth. The UN medium projection assumes that where fertility is very low it will rise again to 1.7-1.9 children per women. In all countries where fertility is currently above replacement level of 2.1, it assumes that it will not fall below that level.

Yet fertility has fallen below replacement level in so many countries, which such different cultures and different stages of economic growth, that is increasingly looking as if low fertility may be here to stay. If this became the case, then world population may peak at some where between 8 and 9 billion. There after it may well begin to decline. The 1996 long range low projection has world population falling to 5.6 billion in 2100 AD.

None of this means that reproductive rights should have lower priority in future. Their contribution to the health and welfare of women and children and clear. Many poor countries in Africa and South Asia face huge population-increases which will be hard to accommodate without major problems of land and water scarcity. In these areas reproductive rights receive a very high priority.

Increasingly our concern must focus on consumption, and how we can cope with the effects of its inexorable increase. Over the past 25 years, world population increased by 53 per cent, but world consumption per person (Measured by income) by only 39 per cent. Assume that consumption per person will rise 100 per cent, while population will rise by only half that amount. As time goes on the preponderance of consumption will increase more and more.

There is a crucial difference between population and consumption aspirations. If fully assured of children's survival most people have quite modest desires for family size. But their desire to consume knows no upper bounds. As wealth increases, people double-up their possessions; two or three cars, two bathrooms, two rooms with all contents, two or three holidays a year.

Appliances improve every year and old ones "need" replacing. New needs are created that never existed before. Globalisation is making products cheaper than ever. TVs are no longer uncommon even in African shanty towns. The number of households is increasing as people live longer and family breakdown becomes more common. Smaller households consume considerably more per cent than large. Moreover, consumption is politically very difficult to restrain. No-one can get elected promising people they can earn and spend less, or re-elected if they fulfil their promises.

In view of this much of the burden of reducing or environment impact will rest on technology. Technology will have to deliver major shifts in improving resource productivity, and in reducing the amount of waste we create. All our institutions and forms of management which affect technology will need to be geared to this end.

In some areas the record has been good and looks likely to remain so. Productivity has kept up with demand in the case of resources that are traded on markets, and that are under the direct control of people or companies affected by shortage or prices. Global food production has kept place with demand: although land and cereal production per person has declined, average intakes of calories and protein have continued to improve and are at record levels. Malnutrition persists, but this is due to poverty and landlessness, not to the inability of the world to produce enough food. We have not encountered any limiting shortage of any key mineral resources or of energy. Nor are we likely to, because we continually economise and find substitutes, there has been a gradual reduction in the material used for each unit of production.

The prospects are much worse for resources that are not traded on markets or subject to sustainable management, as yet. These include groundwater, state forests, ocean fish, bio-diversity in general. They include communal waste sinks like rivers lakes and oceans, and the global atmosphere. In all of these areas it looks likely that things will get quite a lot worse before they get better.

These kinds of resources and sinks are not under the direct control of people affected by shortage or damage. People wishing to change the way a common resource or sink is used or managed have to pass through the legal or political system. They must organize, take out lawsuits against polluters, pressurize legislators and so on. Political responses are typically slow. Usually the majority of voters have to be convinced of the need for action before politicians will risk taking action. Even then powerful and rich vested interests will lobby hard for the status quo, and will often succeed in frustrating changes that are desired by a global majority. America's coal, oil, and car lobbies have stood in the way of any significant US commitment to reduce carbon dioxide output, and the US is the world's largest emitter of carbon dioxide.

Usually there has to be very widespread and very visible environmental damage before action is taken. The thinning of the ozone layer fitted that category well and the response was swift. North Atlantic fishing reached that point in the 1990s, yet politicians shied away from taking adequate action until the last moment: fishing stocks plummeted and there was massive job loss. Global warming is still long way from the damage being widespread enough, and attributable clearly enough to human activities, for politicians to be ready to speed up the move into renewable energy.

The question with the common resources and sinks is always: will be react in time? The answer is all the more difficult because we usually don't know in advance what is "in time." Many critical changes are subject to threshold effects. When a certain point is crossed, very sudden and disastrous change can occur with little warning. In many cases we do not know where the thresholds lie.

Prudence dictates a preventive approach—a stitch in time saves nine. But the history of environmental problems shows that politicians rarely act decisively until the brink is reached, and it will always be touch and go whether we are pushed over it or not.

12

Renewing the State

Many view globalization as a technology driven global order that has led to an intensification of inter-connectedness among nations. This, however, is merely one fact of globalization, and does not presuppose the ideological homogenization or the rapid retrenchment of the welfare state that is currently underway.

The dispute over globalization is not about the intensification of global inter-connectedness. Rather, it is over the vision of the global system that globalization projects. This vision entails a global economic system with identifiable rules of behaviour in trade, finance, taxation, investment policy, intellectual property rights, and currency convertibility, all of which are crafted along neo-liberal principles with minimal governmental regulation. This global system represents a new phase of capitalism which is "more universal, more unchallenged, more pure and more unadulterated than even before".

For many critics, globalization is essentially an anti-democratic process that excludes the interests of a wide range of groups. But the process is not shaped by market forces alone. It is only made possible by the acquiescence if not active support of governments, especially those in advanced countries.

Governments in developing countries, meanwhile, are often said to be unable to stand up to globalization without incurring severe costs. The government of South Africa, for example, could be punished by capital flight if it insists on implementing its agenda of social reform. The masses of South Africa, however, are likely to sustain heavier costs if the government abandons its reforming mandate. Faced with such a dilemma, governments have generally selected the side of capital for a simple reason.

The list of problems caused by globalization is long. In low-income countries, such as those in Sub-Saharan Africa, where governments have been unable or unwilling to provide their populations with even the most basic protection from the new phase of global capitalism and structural adjustment programmes, the people's plight has been particularly severe.

Opponents of globalization are addressing genuine problems. But it is uncertain whether they will succeed in reversing globalization or even in mitigating is adverse impacts. To begin with, many of them are badly organized. Most of them have also rallied around specific issues instead of articulating a comprehensive counter vision. At this point, the counter vision they project appears to be a global system which is not shaped by the narrow interests of capital but which accommodates the interests of diverse social groups. This vision, however, is not yet well developed.

Further more, these opponents have yet to develop viable strategies to constrain globalization. Some argue for weakening or even abolishing institutions such as the World Bank, the International Monetary Fund, and the World Trade Organization, which they view as agents of globalization, it is unclear why business interests and governments would allow this to happen. The relevance of these bodies is only likely to decline if Third World countries, especially middle-income ones, begin to reduce their dependence of them under pressure from their populations.

Yet the main problem faced by these critics is that many of them do not see the relevance of the state. A successful struggle for genuine popular democracy can liberate the state from the grip of corporate and financial interests, turning it into a critical agent for the promotion of board social interests. Many NGOs rely instead of civil society, though this cannot substitute the state is policymaking. The struggle against globalization in essentially a struggle for democracy: the state cannot be bypassed, but must be won.

13

People as Hostages

The Humanitarian Consequences of Sanctions

Following the end of the Cold War, the UN was able to rediscover and impose the sanctions provided for by Article 41 of the UN Charter to maintain or restore international peace and security. Whereas during the preceding decades the UN Security Council had applied such non-military coercive measures only twice, against Rhodesia and South Africa, sanctions have been imposed more than ten times since 1989. The targets: Iraq, Yugoslavia, Somalia, Liberia, Libya, Haiti, Angola, Rwanda, Sudan, Afghanistan, and Sierra Leone. There is now enough experience of the useful and harmful impacts of sanctions to be able to assess the feasibility of this instrument and suggest reforms. That applies also to the bilateral sanctions imposed by the USA.

The Impact of Sanctions

The application of sanctions is at first accompanied with hopes, which are followed mostly by disappointment and sometimes by abhorrence. The hopes are based on the belief that sanctions still can prevent an armed conflict by making a targeted country drop its belligerent attitude due to its leaders listening to reason or responding to the pressure of their people. Disappointment arises from the unreliable calculation of political success, from considerations of legitimacy, and from the problems of affected their countries. Abhorrence is triggered by the ethical dilemma that the suffering caused by sanctions has a greater impact on the ordinary people than upon the political elite, making them hostages to the confrontation.

To be sure, the UN organs, the Security Council is a political rather than a judicial or humanitarian organ of the international community. It does not have to observe the principle of equal treatment and can react differently to developments in Haiti than to those in Nigeria or Burma, to say nothing about Chechnya. But like all UN organs, the Security Council is bound to overarching principles. These include in particular respect for human rights, which it must bear in mind in considering the consequences of its actions.

From a developmental viewpoint, it is worrying to note that sanctions are targeted almost solely on countries of the South. That is just as questionable as the damage suffered by the neighbours and trade partners of countries under sanctions. That applies, for instance, to the Danube littoral states in the case of Yugoslavia, and to Jordan in the case of the sanctions against Iraq.

Furthermore, one of the other drawbacks in wielding the sanctions instrument is the longstanding practice of imposing them on an open-ended basis. That means a country can rid itself of sanctions only with great effort because the veto of a single permanent member of the Security Council can prevent them from being lifted. If sanctions were in future imposed for fixed periods, it would require a fresh Security Council decision to reapply them. Given this process, the sanctions against Libya, for example, would have ended much earlier.

Finally, it is hard to bear that some major powers instrumentalise the Security Council for their own purposes, such as the USA in its quarrel with Libya. Leading Western new media covering the Lockerbie trial in The Netherlands were means-while drip-feeding their publics with selective information from secret service circles to prepare them for the news that Libyan involvement in the bomb blast which brought down the Pan Am airliner over Scotland was unlikely to be proven.

Discussion in the UN

The recommendations of UN secretaries-general for many years for more care in applying the sanctions instrument correspond to a widely held view in the UN. For instance, Boutros Boutros-Ghali called in his annex to the UN's Agenda for Peace of January 1995 for a "mechanism" to assess and examine the consequences of sanctions. And in Kofi Annan's Millennium Report of April 2000, he called on the UN heads of state and government leaders to agree on measures to make economic sanctions adopted by the Security Council impact less harshly on innocent populations, and more effective in bringing pressure to bear on target regimes. The international Red Cross and other humanitarian aid Organisations have for years made similar statements.

First and foremost, it is about avoiding so-called humanitarian consequences. In 1997 the UN did, in fact, cancel implementation of an agreed flight ban against Sudan due to an expert report which forecast such impacts. That is distinct progress. It also shows that as a rule it is not a matter of unforeseen or unintended impacts in the sense of 'collateral damage', but about the acceptance of foreseeable and deliberate consequences. For in contrast to the rules of warfare, which primarily should not be waged against the civil population, the logic of sanction impacts is based on their intended effect on the people of the target country. Their morale is to be broken, making them exert internal pressure on their rulers.

The Case of Iraq

Humanitarian consequences arise above all when comprehensive economic sanctions are imposed which, as in the cases of Iraq and Yugoslavia, ban international trade, transport and financial transactions. That means infant and child mortality, hunger, sickness and human misery: impacts that are visibly and measurably a danger to life.

Certainly, causality in individual cases is an area of dispute. Iraq is a clear example of that. The sanctions against it are affecting a population that in a short time have lived through two terrible and bloody wars involving heavy losses, and whose ruler obviously does not give top priority to the immediate basic needs of his people. So there is more than one reason for the misery. But mutual apportioning of blame can exculpate no-one. Whoever creates conditions that cause innocent children to die cannot with a clear conscience claim that others have done that too. The US and Iraqi governments, however, are so deeply hostile to each other that even taking an objective view of the situation in the interest of the people affected is judged as taking sides.

At any rate, sanctions contribute a great deal to worsen a people's plight. Unfortunately, the international debate on sanctions tends so settle for demanding a guarantee of access for humanitarian aid. The Security Council resolutions contain corresponding exemption provisions. Demarcations in the sector of 'duel use' goods have also become somewhat more sensible since the days when Winston Churchill argued that war material could be made even from food. Foodstuffs and medical supplies are excepted from the embargo. But that does not solve the humanitarian problem. As we unfortunately note constantly, the aid available around the world is not enough to provide sufficient help in all emergency and disaster situations. That means the people of an internationally outlawed country can expect even less assistance.

An especially annoying circumstance in the case of Iraq was that its own rich resources were not allowed to be used for emergency aid. The 'oil-for-food' programme approved by the UN in 1996 was supposed to remedy that to a limited extent. But few people know that only part of the proceeds from Iraq's oil sales is available for humanitarian purposes because sums to compensate victims of Iraq's aggression against Kuwait and pay of UN costs are deducted first. Still, the aid is useful and has resulted in a certain improvement in supply. Whoever reports that much expect censure from those critics of the UN for whom the fact that aid is reaching the people affected does not fit their negative enemy image.

The debate on whether the sanctions against Iraq have led to a threefold of five-fold increase in child mortality can be left to the experts. Rightly, UNICEF, the WHO and others have highlighted these figures because they in particular grab public attention. But one should realize that these statistics are only an indication of the dreadful worsening of the overall health situation of the people of Iraq over the last decade. Before the Gulf war, Iraq was relatively prosperous, its public health service was well staffed and well equipped and able to offer the people comprehensive free healthcare at a good level. It is now totally ruined. Malnutrition and poor drinking water quality have led to an increase in many illnesses on a sometimes-epidemic scale. Hospitals are unable to function due to a lack of equipment and medicines.

The decline of the public health service is in turn also only an indication of the general shortcomings in Iraq that is expressed equally in a run-down school system, widespread unemployment and other social dislocation such as the gradual disappearance of small to medium-sized businesses and an increase in crime.

Reform Proposals are on the Table

Three years ago, a group of American academics presented a list of indicators aimed at helping to establish the starting point and impact of sanctions in the social sector. Among other things, it was meant to point out the vulnerabilities of endangered sections of populations and enable recommendations for the design of sanction regimes. The report offered some telling and cogent indicators for the sectors of public health, the economy, migration movements, politics and humanitarian aid. Most of these indicators were registered by UN specialist organizations. The intention now is to incorporate such information as standards in the consultation and decision processes of the Security Council.

For here it is a question of fundamental human rights which the international community must respect. The people threatened or affected by sanctions have compelling rights (jus cogens). First of all, these are the right to life, good health, food, water, housing and clothing. Starving a people must never be permitted. The limits of sanctions are clearly overstepped when a considerable section of the population drops below the subsistence level. With regard to Iraq, there has been growing criticism in recent years that the Security Council has not met fully its responsibility for the consequences of its actions. The UN's economic sanctions were at any rate from the time that they led to life-threatening impacts for the Iraqi civil population, and in particular to an empirically verifiable reduction of life expectancy due to lack of and under-supply of the people, as well as an increase in child mortality, a violation of the right to life and thus are to be judged as unlawful.

It is morally and legally untenable to treat the people of so-called 'rogue states' inhumanly or to make humanitarian aid subject to political changes, as recently in Yugoslavia. Whoever does that is himself a rogue. Sanctions must not be used, as to date, as what Boutros-Ghali called a "blunt instrument". They should above all hit decision-takers and political elites. 'Smart sanctions' are called for, and are being discussed keenly at international conferences. 'Scalpel rather than a cudgel' is the motto.

14

Who is Responsible for Corruption in Aid?

World Bank President James Wolfensohn's pronouncement that the 'cancer' of corruption seriously undermines development and will not be tolerated in future Bank funded projects prompts one to ask: where and when did this corruption originate? How much corruption is acceptable to the World Bank and donor community? For many years the World Bank tended to ignore or discount the significance of corruption in its operations. Donor agencies in general seem to have a very high tolerance for the misuse of their money. Now that the Bank, the UK system, and bilateral agencies are under growing pressure to improve their performance, they are seeking ways to limit the currupt use of aid money. For the moment, there is little or no evidence that they have any idea of how to go about the task.

One of the main reasons for the disappointing performance of structural adjustment programmes is the misuse of donor money, including systematic corruption. An extreme example is Tanzania's import support programme, which allowed local manufacturers and traders to import raw materials and finished goods. An increasing number of companies, both private and parastatal, began to abuse the system. They stopped paying counterpart funds. Import duty and sales tax were not paid on imports. Neither the Treasury nor the commercial banks had the administrative capacity or the integrity to handle large volumes of free foreign exchange, but the donors ignored the problem. Only when the scandalous behaviour of the banks, the Treasury and the Minister of

Finance had reached epic proportions, fuelling inflation and completely derailing the budgetary process, did the World Bank and other donors finally pull the plug on import support.

In December 1996, the IMF started disbursing US$ 240 million enhanced structural adjustment loan, but to date not one private or parastatal company has been put in receivership for the hundreds of millions of donor dollars which went astray via import support. This casual approach to large-scale corruption has been the norm among donors.

Some bilateral donors have cut the number of countries which they assist, and eradicated funds to those remaining. To increase aid effectiveness some of them have also reduced the number of sectors they support per country. Add to this the tendency for the whole donor community to move into new activities at the same time, and you have a recipe for too much aid chasing too little 'absorptive capacity' in the countries of concentration. Which include Tanzania, Uganda and Kenya, Pressure to spend had led to unbelievable overfunding in certain sectors. Well known examples are NGO's, many of which are created with the sole objective of embezzling donor money.

With the coming of political pluralism, a growing volume of aid money has been channeled into 'governance' activities. The disadvantages of governance from the donor perspective are that donors have little experience in this field, and the amounts of money which can be disbursed, compared to the amount of administrative work involved, are relatively trival.

Aid has served to encourage the establishment of a whole range of corrupt activities in 'civil society' to add to those who already existed in the state apparatus. Many of those managing the corruption are recent migrants from the state sector, or straddle both public and private sectors. The politically acceptable employment of more local personnel as desk officers has served to increase the rate of corruption. The chances of being caught or punished are minimal. The few genuine local change-agents are crowded out by the charlatans and opportunities. The imperative to disburse at all costs makes it very difficult for donors to adequately monitor or evaluate the quality of their assistance, since it would put the agencies in a poor light if they were seen to be supporting non-performing and corrupt activities. Thus, as has generally been the case, the donors pretend that their assistance is being well used, and are even prepared to deny well founded allegations of the misuse of project funds.

The new aid activities discussed above account for a relatively small proportion of total aid flows, however. The basic issue is the amount of uncontrolled corruption which still characterizes the World Bank and other donors' more traditional project, programme, and financial support. Here too one finds projects of ever growing magnitude, as the big spending goes on. The continued availability of donor money is the major determinant of the volume of aid, not performance, structural reform, or impact on 'target groups', Although further project aid cannot be justified on the basis of past performance, it continues to be a major form of aid delivery by both the World Bank and other donor agencies.

The picture which emerges is that of an oppressed people largely at the mercy of an incompetent and corrupt state apparatus. The role of aid in helping to create and reproduce this lamentable state of affairs is worth exploring. Unfortunately, the report does not mention corruption in aid. If corruption has become one of the major international issues of modern times, it would hardly be surprising to find that the virus has already infected and is spreading within the major agencies.

If countries with as much corruption as Tanzania, Uganda, and Kenya can continue to enjoy billions of dollars of aid every year, it is not because they have demonstrated their ability to use aid wisely. But the donors are not well placed to extol the virtues of transparency and accountability which they do not practice themselves. To address the question of corruption in aid, the World Bank and other agencies will have to take a long look at their own role in creating the problem which they now propose to cure.

15

Corruption

Where to Draw the Line?

Everyday the community is being stunned as reports of irregular practices compete for press headlines. The impression is that bribery and corruption, in the form of another is both extensive and increasing; although systematic statistics in this area are rare for obvious reasons.

What is corruption? The list of possibilities is extensive. It starts with the outright bribery of government officials and the more ambiguous question of political contributions; then there are a whole range of activities that could be considered to some degree corrupt—covering such things as the misuse of company assets for political favours, kickbacks and protection money for the police, payola to disc jockeys, sympathetic feature articles in return for advertising revenue, free revenue, free junkets for MP's and journalists, secret price-fixing agreements, obtaining parts in films for reasons not wholly related to acting ability, insider dealing of various kinds, as well as the improper use of the "old boy" network.

All these forms of behaviour have one thing in common. They are attempts to influence the outcome of a decision where the nature of that influence is not made public. Essentially the practices are nothing more or less than the abuse of power.

Reasons for Spread of Corruption

There are several reasons for this spread of corrupt

practices. First the concentration of power in larger and larger units; particularly when combined with rapid growth where the channels of accountability are underdeveloped. It is also widespread in "mature" societies where highly developed networks attempt to preserve the "status-quo" and further their vested interests.

As Gunnar Myrdal, the renowned economist, succinctly put it in his classical study "Asia Drama". "Generally speaking, the habitual practice of bribery and dishonesty tends to pave the way for an authoritarian regime, whose disclosures of currupt practices in the preceding government and whose punitive action against offenders provide a basis for its initial acceptance by the articulate strata of the population".

While corruption inevitable undermines the political system, or organizational structure, in the long run those involved are invariably more concerned with the short term. Also corrupt practices can be infectious. In certain areas companies with high ethical standards have either been forced out of business, or have had to give up their high standards, where their rivals have been willing to pay bribes to win orders.

It is sometimes claimed that "first class" companies are relatively "clean-atleast in the narrow sense—because they can afford to be. They are already powerful and influential, with a network of informal contacts and relationships, so they dod not need to beg and bribe as a way of getting business. It is often the new company trying to break into a new market, or the company fighting for survival, that is the most likely to use bribes to cut corners. Hence the problem is prevelant both in periods of rapid economic growth and change, as well as in periods of economic crisis; although there is some evidence to suggest that more of it might come to the surface, usually by accident, during the latter than former.

It is also occasionally argued—usually not very convincingly—that corruption does not actually impede development but may even accelerate it by helping to by-pass bureaucratic red-tape. However, life is rarely that simple and entrepreneurs within this approach invariably ensure that all too frequently that payments are made and nothing gets done! A recipe for disaster especially as it is somewhat difficult for the aggrieved party to complain under these circumstances.

Unfair Distribution of Income

In some cases it has been known for payments to be strictly calculated as a defined percentage of the expected gain from a legislative concession. While on other occasions payments have become so institutionalized that they are virtually another form of taxation. However, the differences between a "corruption surcharge" and taxation needs to be recognized; the former are rarely made openly, they are usually unfair and rarely are they seen to be fair. In addition they usually redistribute the income in a socially regressive direction.

The important factor appears to be to ensure that, wherever possible, practices and channels of accountability are made public. In practice, there are few absolute principle, and trade-offs are inevitable. The key element is the extent to which any decision is made openly and appears to have wide-spread support. If deals can be kept completely private, the social and political repercussions will, atleast in the short term, be minimal. But anyone working on such an assumption, who then finds his, or her, activities made public, is likely to be in a dangerously exposed position.

In general, companies prefer clear and accepted codes of behaviour—for everyone. But deciding on what is fair competition, as opposed to unfair advantage can be complicated and subjective as both individual and corporate standards of acceptable behaviour are conditioned by the traditions and characteristics of the society in which they operate.

What can be done to eliminate corruption in both its monetary and non-monetary forms? The first step is usually to pass a law making atleast monetary corruption an offence. It is assumed that unaccountable assets are by themselves sufficient evidence of corruption. However, there is little evidence to suggest that the extent of corruption is related to the type of legislation, as the problems of law enforcement are usually formidable in this area.

The paradox at the centre of an anti-corruption programme is that the laws must first be passed by governments and the standards set by politicians are a vital element in this process, yet these are the very people who are most likely to profit from illicit payments.

Of course no measures against corruption are likely to be effective if officials are so badly paid that they cannot live on their salaries. As a result many have combined an anti-corruption programme with an increase in official salaries. Unfortunately, although poor pay frequently drives people to extort bribes higher pay by itself, rarely stops it. This is partly due to the perennial problem that few people consider themselves adequately paid and partly because in both the corporate and political arenas ineffective control systems provide a fertile breeding-ground for the more blatant forms of monetary corruption. In order to reduce these abuses the role of independent auditors needs to be strengthened in almost every country.

It is not altogether surprising that the normal agencies of law enforcement usually find themselves unable to curb, let alone eliminate, corruption. Because of this governments have set up special bodies charged with the task of investigation and enforcing anti corruption legislation. Although sizeable penalties and more independent powers of inquiry are obviously helpful, it is difficult to establish any relationship between the existence of special organizations and the extent of corruption. It does not need emphasizing that these agencies invariably run the risk of concentrating on the more blatant forms of monetary occupation and rarely investigate its more subtle forms. Related to this area is the whole subject of establishing a legitimate basis for "whistleblowing".

Power and Corruption

Corruption tends to be most frequent where governments take on greater powers to bestow special privileges on various sectors of the economy and society. Where there is this concentration of power there is an urgent need to ensure more open accountability. The media is frequently the key to this process of accountability but, unfortunately, it is often either controlled by the authorities, or subject to its own internal pressures from advertisers or other influences. Corruption is the universal disease of the body politic, it varies only in degree and visibility. It is least in extent when the press is free and uncorrupted and when the public are organized sufficiently to demand honest government. It is usually most widespread when the opposite conditions apply. But how often are cases revealed as a result of penetrating investigative journalism, rather than vulture like exposure once the revelation has come to light? And how often do unethical practices come to light from the systematic application of the control machinery, rather than almost by an accident?

Nevertheless, in essence, the problem of corruption is easily solved. If everyone worked on the assumption that whatever they did to influence a decision would be public knowledge, the vast majority of monetary and non-monetary corrupt practices would never arise.

Recent revelations suggest there are signs we are moving away from that utopian state. Yet, if this trend is not controlled and reversed, the consequences for individuals, companies will continue to be extremely serious. It can even lead to a crisis of confidence in the system itself.

For all these reasons it is not surprising to find that Ethics is now one of the most rapidly expanding subject areas everywhere.

16

What was the Wrong with Structural Adjustment?

In Defence of a Much-Maligned Strategy

After decades of stranded development theories, ideologies and paradigms, "structural adjustment", with its demands for clean fiscal policy and an end to uneconomic state enterprises, political privileges, market and exchange rate intervention and corruption, entered the aid arena like a refreshing dawn after a long night of frustrating dreams. Only the "old guard" of planned economy advocates and jealous academicians who had missed the boat were able to shut their eyes to the moral and economic justification of this liberating break-through in international development policy spearheaded by the Breton Woods institutions then steered by some exceptionally courageous economists.

Reaction to SAPS

As with any revolution, defeat is awaiting the pioneers at the hands of political power agreed, reactionary tactics by the formerly privileged and academic envy. The principal device serving the reactionary forces as a lever of influence on the mood of the "development community" has been the identification and dramatization of new pockets or strata of (principally urban) poverty allegedly created by structural adjustment measures, while shunning the much broader-based rise in economic activity, real incomes and sense of fair reward in the overall society, especially the rural population. That the hardship experienced by urban poor, formerly privileged under consumer price control and import subsidies to the debit of depressed farm prices or maintained by grossly over-expanded public payrolls, was only laying open the camouflaged erosion of the economy and near-bankruptcy of governments and public enterprises was conveniently downplayed.

These reactionary howls were to be expected. Not that they met the entirely innocent. There had been naively sweeping, overly assuming demands by some structural adjustment missions. But an intellectually vigorous and dynamic "development community" would have coped with the ensuing opposition, strengthened the analytical and monitoring capacities and the political will to endure also rocky roads and bitter medicines on the way to a healthier base. Instead, institutional rivalry, political opportunism and emotive populism were thriving. In a way, the "development community" behaved as if it did not want its patient to become able to stand on his own feet and eventually steal its raison d'etre.

Worst, the Bretton Woods institutions themselves, partly under the pressure of the emotive opposition described above fell to the temptation to rescue their lending volume, which was threatened by the frugality dictated to third World public budgets under structural adjustment recipes, through hardship-easing loans. They thereby corrupted their creation in using it to reinforce their indispensability. As a consequence it soon turned out that some of the most obedient loan takers under structural adjustment terms experienced sharply rising indebtedness, exploited as a disqualifying symptom by the anti-structural adjustment camp.

Whatever the opinions on structural adjustment policies, the commitment to the principles of "good governance" has come to stay, at least on paper, as an almost standard conditionally for official development aid from OECD donor countries. The realization, matured in the implementation of structural adjustment programmes, that not the quantity of aid, but the quality of Third World governments determines the positive or negative course of development, may be regarded as the most valuable fruit of the decades-old-policy debate in the 'development community'. And the use of aid as a pressure or bribing factor towards "good governance" as foreign aid's least disputable purpose.

Out of the Limelight

Nothing, however, must be taken for granted. Achievement breads its challenge! Structural adjustment, though in essence hardly disputable has been pushed out of the limelight and replaced by the oldest actor in the company: eradication of poverty, twinned with an equally perpetual endeavour at the macro-level: debt-forgiveness. This falling back to square one in donors' approach to the problems of the south, i.e., the call to alleviate poverty and priorities direct efforts to this end above all other developmental efforts—does it indicate a sell-out of constructive ideas in the 'development community'? Has any noteworthy progress been achieved in the past by this approach?

By telling a frugally toiling but independent subsistence farmer that internationally his condition is classed as "poverty", deserving compassion and support by the world community and cancellation of his debts, one can hardly expect a sustainable improvement in his output, satisfaction, or self-respect and even less, when he realizes that the help principally provides jobs, fringe benefits and self-importance to a gamut of intermediaries, at home and abroad.

What do those poverty advocates (the "lords of poverty") really know about the resources, life management, value systems and ambitions of those they generalize by the billions? The great variance in the conception of life situations, from different external viewpoints.

What the aid system can do for these rural populations classed as "poor"/"underprivileged"/"exploited", is press for justice, i.e., "good governance". The achievements of structural adjustment policy through e.g., abolishing official price and exchange rate distortions, import subsidies and exploitative state agencies, has brought massive income improvement for peasant populations, i.e., the majority of LDC inhabitants, in dimensions unreachable by whatsoever direct "attack" on rural "poverty". What people want is not being benevolently treated as poor, but being justly rewarded for their work, i.e., by access to the unmanipulated market value of their output. Slackening on structural adjustment/"good governance" conditionally under the present "10 year itch" for paradigm change means foregoing much of the potential opportunities for undoing injustice and exploitation of the masses. It should be clear where priority focus should be placed in ODA policy.

Small is not Beautiful

The direct attack on "poverty", orchestrated by the Bretton Woods institutions under their freshly launched Poverty Reduction Strategy Paper (PRSP) campaign, is being rightly regarded as primarily an NGO domain, since most activities are expected to be carried out at local community level. This would require careful screening and coordinating of NGO activities and their integration via gradual expansion of their experience. But "small" is not "beautiful" for the development financing institutions. Disbursement needs are pressing, calling for the new paradigm to quickly provide channels for another wave of loans to the "IDA Countries". Their problem of heavy indebtedness, which would principally exclude most of them from any new loan consideration, shall be solved with one stroke (which only the well-cushioned development bureaucracy can afford); debt relief against presentation of country PRSPs by the respective governments. NGOs are expected to play in the system especially the knowledge gap about the "poor" people's real wants and needs NGOs will naturally be tempted by such expansionary boost to their involvement (referred to sarcastically as their philanthropic empire" by an African conference participant), but this will not be conducive to quality and accountability of their performance, which ideally should be based on private sponsorship in combination with strong target-group provided self-help components.

Patience and Self-Restraint

Local knowledge and initiatives cannot be obtained under time pressure. "The grass does not grow faster by being pulled". When will be "development community" learn patience and self-restraint in the approach to LDC's capacity for constructive absorption of aid programmes accompanied by a genuine sense of ownership?

After all these deliberations, how shall development policy be shaped in order to better correspond with reality, without sinking deeper into hypocrisy and frustration?

To come back to the opening question: what was wrong with "structural adjustment"? Nothing was wrong with its intent. In fact this was very right and long overdue. Its implementation, however, lacked patience, perseverance and solid support from the development community, apart from its being corrupted as a vehicle for expansionary lending policy. If aid is mean to not be an end in itself, then structural adjustment policy needs constant reinforcement, underpinned by strict lending discipline. There should be an end to irresponsible lending and easy escape from its consequences by wholesome periodic debt relief burdened on the international tax-paying community. No ODA, either loans or grants, should be made available to governments who are not in active process of implementing "good governance" principles. A monitoring unit, reporting to the donor community on government performance in regard to its "good government"? Structural adjustment commitment, should be maintained in each and receiving country by "donor consortia" comprising all locally represented bilateral and multilateral development organizations currently extending technical, financial or material assistance to the country.

In order to accommodate the poverty focus without diluting the necessary structural adjustment orientation of ODA, a division of activity-focus between the latter and the NGO sector would seen to be advantageous.

- ODA, limited to the countries abiding to structural adjustment/"good governance" conditionally, with focus concentration on sustainable physical, social and economic infrastructure principally at national and regional level, public management training, higher education and research, consultant and senior adviser services.

- The NGO sector, principally funded by private sponsorship, united to structural adjustment conditionally (but preferably grafted on local self-help initiative), with focus-concentration on the "third World" "poor", i.e., mostly at rural community and law-income township level, for amelioration of living conditions and local resource utilization.
- strengthening of linkages between the NGO sector and the UN Technical Agencies to mutual benefit: NGOs in need of professional information, evaluation and advice or forum for discussion to find an actively supportive window at the agencies; the latter to maintain and develop field contact for research and policy generation, not least as a substitute for their declining project work (giving way to greater concentration on their global functions i.e., serving as information, policy initiation, and coordination/negotiation center on topics of global concern, such as e.g.; human rights, global monetary and trade systems, tropical forest and global marine resources, global and Regional health threats, international standards.)

In conclusion, it may be called to mind that aid and its institutions have no claim for permanence. They are justified only as temporary functions in a phasing-out process of self-help support. Any claim for unlimited continuity would breed lasting infantilisation.

17

Venture Capital for Small and Medium Business

A Proposal for South-South Cooperation

Although great strides have been made in the last decade to help finance business start-ups for micro-enterprises in low-income countries (LICs) using models such as the Grameen Bank in Bangladesh and others, on similar initiative has been taken to help small and medium enterprises (SMEs) in these countries.

Development banks or other development finance institutions (DFIs) in developing countries are not really meant nor organized to serve the particular needs of their counties' SMEs. They are not only unable to draw on a local capital market to finance their operations, but they also lack the range of advisory services required by SMEs to submit bankable loan applications and are themselves ill-equipped to evaluate such applications. Consequently, they concentrate on a few large projects—preferably of the infrastructure type—for which they rely on the technical expertise of the foreign donors financing them or specially hired consultants.

In the absence of a realistic access to DFIs, SMEs have been constrained to seek their loans for new business ventures from commercial banks. The fact that since 1978 the World Bank has been challenging a large portion of its credit lines intended for SMEs through commercial banks rather than through DFIs, reflects the importance with donors attach to the role of LIC commercial banks as the principal intermediaries for SME lending.

Reasons for Failure of Traditional Banking Systems

However, there are several important reasons why commercial banks are ill-suited to perform this task. First and foremost, the banking systems of these countries were conceived during a period when most investment capital was provided by the government, usually drawing on foreign aid. Thus, even in those LICs which had not entirely succumbed to the socialist ideology in the sense of eliminating all private enterprise, commercial banks continue to limit their credit activity largely to self-liquidating, law-risk credits seldom exceeding 12 month's duration, preferably conventional trade credits. Secondly, even in the exceptional cases where commercial banks in these countries entertain applications for medium-term credits to finance the launching of a small manufacturing project, they will normally demand ironclad collateral in the forms of liens on real-estate and/or personal guarantees by friends and relatives with similar backing, unless and applicant is a well-known customer of the bank.

Thirdly, with their overriding concern for profitability, most LIC commercial banks tend to like upon business start-up loans to SMEs as being too risky and/or administratively too costly to handle in relation to the loan amounts involved. For these reasons, commercial banks in these countries are unlikely to establish in-house facilities to meet the specific needs of SMEs, such as helping them in project preparation and market analysis. Last but not least, factors such as the project's development orientation" (e.g. its important substitution and export potential, its ability to increase productivity and its employment generation features) do not enter into the calculations of commercial banks which will orient their actions towards "bottom line" results and risk minimization. Under the circumstances, most commercial banks are not inclined to become directly involved in project supervision, as long as their customer's repayment records are satisfactory.

Credit for SMEs

Whereas new approaches have been developed over the last decade by various development assistance agencies to help up-grade commercial banks' staff capability, especially in advising SME borrowers in such matters as project formulation and market analysis as well as improving and market analysis as well as improving their loan repayment capacity, only recently has an effort been made to find ways and means of making investment capital available to SME entrepreneurs for launching new businesses. In some LICs, lines of credit have been established by multilateral or bilateral banks from which loan capital can be sought for such projects, but only; seldom has genuine risk (i.e., equity) capital been made available and when some only; through the donors' own agencies. The interest rate changed by the local banks for administering loans from these credit lines in local currency are generally; at a par with existing commercial rates, which tend to be prohibitive for a new venture of the type being promoted. These high rates are due to several factors, including (a) the local rates of inflation and the consequent devaluation risks, (b) the high risk factor of the new enterprises with little or no collateral and credit standing, and (c) the lack of experience of bank staff in the evaluation of loan requests submitted to them for unfamiliar projects. Significantly, most international DFIs are loath to lower interest rates to be applied on loans financed by their credit lines, lest they be accused of unfair competition on the local financial markets.

Incentives Ineffective in Attracting Foreign Investors

Although may international conferences, investment promotion meetings and other fora have been staged by UN bodies and donor groups to generate private investor interest in the LICs, these efforts have proved largely ineffectual. While much has been done by LIC governments in recent years to create a more attractive "enabling environment" for private investment, these incentives have been necessary but not sufficient to convince developed-country enterprises or investors to assume the necessary risks, with the exception of selected sectors such as mineral extraction, tourism and a narrow range of exportable consumer goods, such as out-of-season fruits and vegetables, and tropical products such as cocoa and certain spices. Even public support for project preparation has ultimately failed to provide preparation has ultimately failed to provide private business in industrial countries the incentives needed to take an active role in a broadly-based economic development of LICs.

The bottom line for potential investors in LICs is constituted by the profits which their investment will yield within a reasonable period of time, under conditions which offer a reasonable amount of political and legal stability. So far, these basic conditions have not been met on the whole. In the new global economy with its almost total reliance on free market principles and the ability to choose investment sites freely, the choice is not likely to fall on the LICs, but rather on a small number of more advanced developing countries, apart from the industrial countries themselves.

South-to-South Technological/Commercial Cooperation

While the inherent disadvantages faced by LICs in competing for foreign investment capital are too great to be overcome by a magic panacea, any attempt at a solution must include measures designed to mobilize the entrepreneurial abilities and dynamism available in existing and potential SMEs engaged in production of a variety of goods destined for the broad consumer market at home and abroad. In most LICs such existing or potential SMEs need to access affordable foreign technologies, i.e., the machinery and the technological know-how required to install and make the machinery function. One of the prime sources of such technologies for LICs can be found in enterprises in South./Southeast Asia and China, countries that have only recently graduated from the LIC status (or have not yet done so but have nevertheless managed to create a modern industrial sector within their overall state of underdevelopment and poverty). The concretization of transfers of technology from these countries to the LICs is especially affected by the financing problems described above, because in the normal case neither one of the potential partners can afford and necessary venture, even though they can and will invest their know-how, time and very often land, buildings and infrastructure. This problems is must less acute in the case of the more expensive, and hence often unaffordable "Northern" technologies, where the technology provider finds it easier to mobilize start-up capital from its own resources or by; borrowing from his commercial bank against his firms' overall credit line.

The underlying economic rationale in favour of such South-to-South, company-to-company transfers of production technology argues that Asian firms can help launch industrial start-ups in these countries far more cheaply and quickly than the more sophisticated companies from the North. By offering labour-intensive rather than capital-intensive production machinery accompanied by vitally needed on the-job training, back-up managerial and maintenance follow-up at a fraction of the cost of Northern firms, Asian companies' cooperation can spell the difference between a successful business start-up and a failed one. Furthermore Asian-sourced machinery can be operated at production scales corresponding to the reduced market requirements and limited purchasing power of most LIC markets.

In view of the above described financing problems faced by South-to-South deals, it is proposed that a Venture Capital fund be established specializing in the provision of equity capital for joint ventures (JVs) among SMEs in various LICs. In many cases the existence of such a FUND—which might be called the VENTURE CAPITAL FUND or simply (VENCAP)—will spell the difference between business proposals that are still-born for want of the required initial financing, and profitable ventures which are launched thanks to the missing—if minority—equity contribution from the FUND.

Characteristics of the FUND

The proposed VENCAP would be expected to be an active participant in the project in which it will invest, sharing its financial and strategic vision with the invest firm. To this end, it must have access to experience project evaluation specialists with intimate knowledge of conditions in low-income countries in general, and the project and its promoters in particular. As might be expected, the FUND would concentrate its resources in early-state financing, rather than in plant expansion or replacement, inasmuch as the projects likely to be the most profitable are the new ones, which will normally start from empty factory buildings and offices, where only a minimum amount of production equipment, if any, is normally usable for the operation of the new JV.

The FUND would limit its participation to joint ventures in which firms of at least two developing countries hold equity stakes, although firms from developed countries might also participate. The fund would limit its participation to production JVs whose total initial capital would not exceed a given sum to be determined. Its own participation would in turn also be limited by a relative ceiling per venture i.e., a maximum percentage of the total capital. This combination would implicitly set an absolute ceiling to the FUND's participation in any given JV.

Success and Selection Criteria

The number of proposed projects must be sufficient to allow the FUND to pick and choose the best. A good ratio of applications to acceptances might be in the range of 10:1. Whereas commercial viability will constitute the first and foremost selection criterion, every effort would be made to select projects which have a strong development character, are environmentally friendly and/or involve production technologies which are deemed to be vital and critical to the recipient country's current socio-economic needs. Thus, preference would be given to sectors such as (a) food processing (b) water purification, (c) renewable energy (d) agricultural development, and (e) light engineering. In all cases, the emphasis would be on cost-effective, labour-intensive production technologies.

The FUND's ability to divest itself of its participation at a profit will be the ultimate test of the FUND's success. Ideally, the FUND should be able to do this within a maximum of one or two years, so as to enable it to effectively cycle its resources to other equally meritorious projects.

Proposals for VENCAP's Organization Structure

Besides being run by an experienced FUND manager, VENCAP would be assisted in its investment decisions by National Advisory Committees (NACs), which would be established in all participating LICs and would be composed of prominent business persons, professional men and women and financiers. These NACs would be chaired by an experienced consultant/consulting firm selected by the FUND. No member of the NAC having business or family links with the person or firm applying for equity financing would participate in the evaluation procedure. VENCAP would be represented on the Boards of Directors of the firms in which it has acquired minority stakes through one or several members of the relevant; NAC. The FUND itself would be run by a Board of Directors in which all of the major investors would be represented (and possibly some NGOs, PVOs).

Follow-up

It is hoped that this article will provoke sufficient interest to justify the convening of an international meeting of aid agency officials and experts to study the ideas set forth above, so as to facilitate VENCAP's formal launching as an operative force. The need is there, the customers are there, the goodwill is there, only the financing and the organization are lacking!

18

The Uruguay Round and Agricultural Reform

The Uruguay Round of Multilateral Trade Negotiations (completed in 1994) continued the process of reducing trade barriers achieved in seven previous rounds of negotiations. Among the Uruguay Rounds's most significant accomplishments were the adoption of new rules governing agricultural trade policy, the establishment of disciplines on the use of sanitary and Phytosanitary (SPS) measures, and agreement on a new process for settling trade disputes. The Uruguay Round also created the World Trade Organization (WTO) to replace the General Agreement on Tariffs and Trade (GATT) as an institutional framework for overseeing trade negotiations and adjudicating trade disputes. Agricultural trade concerns that have come to the fore since the Uruguay Round, including the use of genetically engineered products in agricultural trade, state trading, and a large number of potential new members, illustrate the wide range of issues any new round may face.

During the past years since initial implementation of the Uruguay Round agreements, the round with respect to agriculture is mixed. The Uruguay Round's overall impact on agricultural trade can be considered positive in moving toward several key goals, including reducing agricultural export subsidies, establishing new rules for agricultural import policy, and agreeing on disciplines for sanitary and Phytosanitary trade measures. The Uruguay Round Agreement on Agriculture (URAA) may also have contributed to a shift in domestic support of agriculture away from those practices with the largest potential to affect production and, therefore, to affect trade flows. However, significant reductions in most agricultural tariffs will have to await a future round of negotiations.

Tariffs, Incentives, and Subsidies

Prior to Uruguay Round, trade in many agricultural products was unaffected by the tariff cuts that were made for industrial products in previous rounds. In the Uruguay Round, participating countries agreed to convert all non-tariff agricultural trade barriers to tariffs (a process called "tariffication") and to reduce them. However, agricultural tariffs remain very high for some products in some countries, limiting the trade benefits to be derived from the new rules. To ensure that historical trade levels were maintained and to create some new trade opportunities where trade had been largely precluded by policies, countries instituted tariff-rate quotas. A tariff-rate quota applies a lower tariff to imports below a certain quantitative limit (quota) and permits a higher tariff on imported goods after the quota has been reached.

The Agreement on Agriculture required countries to reduce outlays on domestic policies that provide direct economic incentives to producers to increase resource use or production. All WTO member countries are meeting their commitments to reduce these outlays, and most countries reduced this type of support by more than the required amount. However, support from those domestic policies considered to have the least effect on production, such as domestic food aid, has increased from 1986-88 levels.

In the Agreement on Agriculture, 25 countries that employed export subsidies agreed to reduce the volume and value of their subsidized exports over a specified implementation period. To date, most of these countries have met their commitments, Although some have found way to circumvent them. The European Union (EU) is by far the largest user of export subsidies, accounting for 84 per cent of subsidy outlays of the 25 countries in 1995 and 1996. Despite substantial progress in reducing export subsidies, rising world grain supplies and falling world grain prices will make it difficult for some countries to meet future commitments unless they adopt policy changes.

The Uruguay Round's SPS agreement imposed disciplines on the use of measures to protect human, animal, and plant life and health from foreign pests, diseases, and contaminants. The agreement can be credited with increasing the transparency of countries SPS regulations and providing improved means for settling SPS-related trade disputes, including some important cases involving agricultural products. The agreement has also spurred regulatory reforms in some countries. The SPS agreement and the Agreement on Technical barriers to Trade could provide a framework for disputes over genetically modified organisms (GMOs) brought to the WTO for arbitration.

Current Issues

Changes made to the multilateral dispute resolution process in the Uruguay Round may be as important to agricultural trade as the improvement in the substantive rules governing trade in agricultural goods. Initial evidence indicates that the WTO dispute settlement system is a significant improvement over its GATT predecessor. For example, a single country can no longer block the formation of a dispute resolution panel or veto an adverse ruling by blocking the adoption of a panel report. These improvements have led to a number of important agricultural trade cases being adjudicated before the WTO. The outstanding question for the WTO is whether members who practices have been successfully challenged under the new dispute settlement procedures will live up to their obligations.

Other agriculture-related issues, including a bid for membership by a large and diverse group of potential new WTO members, the challenge of dealing with state trading enterprises (STEs) within WTO disciplines, and issues particular to developing countries, will shape the agenda for future agricultural trade liberalization discussions. Thirty countries are currently seeking membership in the 134-member WTO. Countries seeking WTO membership accede under conditions negotiated with WTO membership through the privileged trade status with WTO member but may incur adjustment costs in reforming their trade policies and reducing tariffs to meet WTO requirements. Current WTO members gain greater access to the markets of acceding countries.

State trading enterprises, governmental and non-governmental entities that have been granted special rights or privileges through which they can influence trade, continue to be important to the trade of agricultural commodities because many countries consider them to be an appropriate means to meet domestic agricultural poli: objectives. Continuing concerns about the trade practices of state trading enterprises in some WTO members countries and the potential accession of China and other countries where STEs are prominent will keep STEs on the WTO agenda.

Developing countries received special treatment in the Uruguay Round, including less stringent disciplines in reforming their trade policies than those apply to developed countries. In the next round of multilateral agricultural trade negotiations, developing countries will continue to have their own interests in the areas of special and differential treatment, export restraints, price stability, food security, food aid, and stock policies. As developing countries identify their positions, coalitions of countries with common trade interests may emerge.

Bibliography

De Soto, H., 1990. *The Other Path: The Invisible Revolution in the Third World.* Reprint edition. New York: Harper Collins.

Doha Development Agenda, 2001. The Ministerial Declaration and other Decisions and Declarations from the Doha Ministerial Conference, Available: http://www.wto.org/English/tratop_e/dda_e/dda_e.htm.

English, P., B. Hoekman, and A. Mattoo, 2002. *Development, Trade and the WTO: A Handbook.* The World Bank, Washington D.C.

Feketekuty, G., 1988, *International Trade in Services: An Overview and Blueprint for Negotiations.* Cambridge, MA: American Enterprise Institute/Ballinger.

Finger, J.M., 1993. *Antidumping: How it Works and Who Gets Hurt.* Ann Arbor: Univ. of Michigan Press.

———, 2001, "Implementing the Uruguay Round Agreements: Problems for Developing Countries." *The World Economy* 24 (9, September): 1097-108.

Finger, J.M. and J.J. Nogues, 2001. The Unbalanced Uruguay Round Outcome: The New Areas in Future WTO Negotiations. Policy Research Working Paper No. 2732, The World Bank, Washington, D.C.

Finger, J.M. and L. Schuknecht, 2001. "Market Access Advances and Retreats: The Uruguay Round and Beyond." In B. Hoekman and W. Martin, eds., *Developing Countries and the WTO: A Pro-active Agenda.* Oxford: UK and Malden. Also available as Policy Research Working Paper No. 2232 at http://www.worldbank.org/research/trade.

Finger, J.M. and P. Schuler, 2000. "Implementation of Uruguay Round Commitments: The Development Challenge." *The World Economy* 23(4, April): 511-25. Also available as Policy Research Working Paper No. 2215 at http://www.worldbank.org/research/trade.

Finger, J.M. and L.A. Winters, 2002. "Reciprocity." In P. English, B. Hoekman, and A. Mattoo, *Development, Trade and the WTO: A Handbook.* The World Bank, Washington D.C.

Finger, J.M., M.D. Ingco, and U. Reincke, 1996. *The Uruguay Round: Statistics on Tariff Concessions Given and Received.* The World Bank, Washington, D.C.

Finger, J.M., F. Ng, and S. Wangchuk, 2001. Antidumping as safeguard Policy. Policy Research Working Paper No. 2730, The World Bank, Washington, D.C.

Francois, J.F., B. McDonald, and H. Nordstrom, 1996. "The Uruguay Round: A Numerically Based Qualitative Assessment." In W. Martin And L.A. Winters, eds., *The Uruguay Round and the Developing Countries:* Cambridge: Cambridge University Press.

Harrison, G.W., T.F. Rutherford, and D.G. Tarr, 1996. "Quantifying the Uruguay Round." In W. Martin and L.A. Winters., Eds., *The Uruguay Round and the Developing Countries.* Cambridge: Cambridge University Press.

Hudec, R.E., 1970. "The GATT Legal System: A Diplomat's Jurisprudence." *Journal of World Trade Law* 4: 615-65.

International Intellectual Property Alliance (IIPA), 2002a. "Description of the IIPA. "Available: http://www.iipa.com/aboutiipa.html.

———, 2002b. "Statististics." Available: http/www.iipa.com/statistics.html.

Martin, W. and L.A. Winters, 1996. *The Uruguay Round and the Developing Countries.* Cambridge: Cambridge University Press.

Martin, W. and L.A. Winters, 1996. "The Uruguay Round: A Milestone for the Developing Countries." In W. Martin L.A. Winters, eds., *The Uruguay Round and the Developing Countries.* Cambridge: Cambridge University Press.

Maskus, K.E., 2000. *Intellectual Property Rights in the Global Economy.* Institute for International Economics. Washington, D.C.

Michalopoulos, C., 1999. "The Developing Countries in WTO." *The World Economy* 22(1) January.

O'Neill, T. And G. Hymel (contributor), 1995. *All Politics is Local: And Other Rules of the Game.* Reprint edition. Massachusetts: Adams Media Corporation.

Panagariya, A., Forthcoming. "Developing Countries at Doha: A Political Economy Analysis". *The World Economy.*

Petersen, M. and D.G. McNeil Jr., 2001. "Maker Yielding Patent in Africa for AIDS Drug" *The New York Times.* 15 March. Page 1.

Preeg, E.H., 1995. *Traders in a Brave New World.* Chicago and London: University of Chicago Press.

Reichman, J.H., 1998. "Securing Compliance with the TRIPS Agreement after US v India." *Journal of International Economic Law* 1(4, December): 603-06.

Ricupero, R., 2000. "A Development Round: Converting Rhetoric into Substance." Paper presented at the Symposium on Efficiency, Euqity and Legitimacy: The Multilateral Trading System at the Millennium, 1-2 June, John F. Kennedy School of Government. Harvard University, Cambridge, Massachusetts.

Shaffer, G., 2002. "The Law-in Action of International Trade Litigation: The Blurring of the Public and the Private." University of Wisconsin Law School, Madison. Manuscript.

Winham, G., 1986. *International Trade and the Tokyo Round of Negotiations.* Princeton: Princeton University Press.

Winters, L.A., 2002. "Doha and the World Poverty Targets." Paper prepared for the Annual Bank Conference on Development Economics (ABCDE), 29-30 April, World Bank, Washington, D.C.

World Bank, 2002. *Global Economic Prospects and the Developing Countries.* The World Bank, Washington D.C.

World Trade Organization (WTO), 2002a. "WTO Secretariat Budget for 2002." Available: http://www.wto.org/English/thewto_e/secre_e/budget_e.htm.

———, 2002b. Pledging Conference to provide sound financial basis for Doha Agenda. Available: http://www.wto.org/English/news_e/pres02_e/pr277_e.htm.

Zeller, T.W., 1992. *American Trade and Power in the 1960s.* New York: Columbia.

Index